HERSHEY'S®

Best-Loved Recipes

Publications International, Ltd.
Favorite Brand Name Recipes at www.fbnr.com

All recipes developed and tested by the Hershey Kitchens.

Front cover photography by Stephen Hamilton Photographics, Inc.

Pictured on the front cover: Chocolate Cake Square with Eggnog Sauce *(page 356)*.

Pictured on the back cover *(left to right):* Cherry Glazed Chocolate Torte *(page 6);* Sweetheart Chocolate Mousse *(page 152);* Royal Hot Chocolate *(page 310),* Mocha Shake *(page 312)* and Luscious Cocoa Smoothie *(page 310).*

ISBN: 0-7853-4958-8

Library of Congress Catalog Card Number: 00-105288

Manufactured in China.

8 7 6 5 4 3 2 1

Nutritional Analysis: Nutritional information is given for [some of] the recipes in this publication. Each analysis is based on the food items in the ingredient list, except ingredients labeled as "optional" or "for garnish." When more than one ingredient choice is listed, the first ingredient is used for analysis. If a range for the amount of an ingredient is given, the nutritional analysis is based on the lowest amount. Foods offered as "serve with" suggestions are not included in the analysis unless otherwise stated.

Microwave Cooking: Microwave ovens vary in wattage. Use the cooking times as guidelines and check for doneness before adding more time.

Preparation/Cooking Times: Preparation times are based on the approximate amount of time required to assemble the recipe before cooking, baking, chilling or serving. These times include preparation steps such as measuring, chopping and mixing. The fact that some preparations and cooking can be done simultaneously is taken into account. Preparation of optional ingredients and serving suggestions is not included.

CONTENTS

1½ cups chocolate cookie crumbs

6 tablespoons butter or margarine, melted

1¼ cups HERSHEY'S MINI KISSES Semi-Sweet Baking Pieces, divided

4 packages (8 ounces each) cream cheese, softened

⅔ cup sugar

3 eggs

⅓ cup milk

1 tablespoon instant espresso powder

¼ teaspoon ground cinnamon

Espresso Cream (recipe follows)

Cappuccino Kissed Cheesecake

Makes 16 servings

1. Heat oven to 350°F. Combine cookie crumbs and butter; press onto bottom and 1 inch up side of 9-inch springform pan.

2. Melt 1 cup Mini Kisses in small saucepan over low heat, stirring constantly. Combine cream cheese and sugar in large bowl, beating on medium speed of mixer until well blended. Add eggs, milk, espresso powder and cinnamon; beat on low speed until well blended. Add 1 cup melted Mini Kisses; beat on medium speed 2 minutes. Spoon mixture into crust.

3. Bake 55 minutes. Remove from oven to wire rack. Cool 15 minutes; with knife, loosen cake from side of pan. Cool completely; remove side of pan. Cover; refrigerate at least 4 hours before serving.

4. To serve, garnish with Espresso Cream and remaining ¼ cup Mini Kisses. Cover; refrigerate leftover cheesecake.

Espresso Cream: Beat ½ cup cold whipping cream, 2 tablespoons powdered sugar and 1 teaspoon instant espresso powder until stiff

4

Cappuccino Kissed Cheesecake

½ cup (1 stick) butter or
     margarine, melted

1 cup granulated sugar

1 teaspoon vanilla extract

2 eggs

½ cup all-purpose flour

⅓ cup HERSHEY'S Cocoa

¼ teaspoon baking powder

¼ teaspoon salt

1 package (8 ounces) cream
     cheese, softened

1 cup powdered sugar

1 cup frozen non-dairy
     whipped topping, thawed

1 can (21 ounces) cherry pie
     filling, divided

CHERRY GLAZED CHOCOLATE TORTE

Makes 10 to 12 servings

1. Heat oven to 350°F. Grease bottom of 9-inch springform pan.

2. Stir together butter, granulated sugar and vanilla in large bowl. Add eggs; using spoon, beat well. Stir together flour, cocoa, baking powder and salt; gradually add to egg mixture, beating until well blended. Spread batter into prepared pan.

3. Bake 25 to 30 minutes or until cake is set. (Cake will be fudgey and will not test done.) Remove from oven; cool completely in pan on wire rack.

4. Beat cream cheese and powdered sugar in medium bowl until well blended; gradually fold in whipped topping, blending well. Spread over top of cake. Spread 1 cup cherry pie filling over cream layer; refrigerate several hours. With knife, loosen cake from side of pan; remove side of pan. Cut into wedges; garnish with remaining pie filling. Cover; refrigerate leftover dessert.

Cherry Glazed Chocolate Torte

2 cups sugar

1¾ cups all-purpose flour

¾ cup HERSHEY'S Cocoa *or* HERSHEY'S Dutch Processed Cocoa

1½ teaspoons baking powder

1½ teaspoons baking soda

1 teaspoon salt

2 eggs

1 cup milk

½ cup vegetable oil

2 teaspoons vanilla extract

1 cup boiling water

"Perfectly Chocolate" Chocolate Frosting (page 10)

HERSHEY'S "PERFECTLY CHOCOLATE" CHOCOLATE CAKE

Makes 8 to 10 servings

1. Heat oven to 350°F. Grease and flour two 9-inch round baking pans.*

2. Stir together sugar, flour, cocoa, baking powder, baking soda and salt in large bowl. Add eggs, milk, oil and vanilla; beat on medium speed of mixer 2 minutes. Stir in water. (Batter will be thin.) Pour batter evenly into prepared pans.

3. Bake 30 to 35 minutes or until wooden pick inserted in center comes out clean. Cool 10 minutes; remove from pans to wire racks. Cool completely.

4. Prepare "Perfectly Chocolate" Chocolate Frosting; spread between layers and over top and side of cake.

One 13×9×2-inch baking pan may be substituted for 9-inch round baking pans. Prepare as directed above. Bake 35 to 40 minutes. Cool completely in pan on wire rack. Frost as desired.

continued on page 10

9

Hershey's "Perfectly Chocolate" Chocolate Cake

Hershey's "Perfectly Chocolate" Chocolate Cake, continued

"PERFECTLY CHOCOLATE" CHOCOLATE FROSTING

Makes about 2 cups frosting

- ½ cup (1 stick) butter or margarine
- ⅔ cup HERSHEY'S Cocoa
- 3 cups powdered sugar
- ⅓ cup milk
- 1 teaspoon vanilla extract

1. Melt butter. Stir in cocoa. Alternately add powdered sugar and milk, beating to spreading consistency.

2. Add small amount of additional milk, if needed. Stir in vanilla.

HERSHEY'S HINT

Bloom, the gray film that sometimes appears on chocolate and chocolate chips, occurs when chocolate is exposed to uneven temperatures or has been stored in damp conditions. Bloom does not affect the taste or quality of the chocolate.

2 cups sugar

1¾ cups all-purpose flour

¾ cup HERSHEY'S Cocoa

1½ teaspoons baking powder

1½ teaspoons baking soda

1 teaspoon salt

2 eggs

1 cup milk

½ cup vegetable oil

2 teaspoons vanilla extract

1 cup boiling water

1 can (21 ounces) cherry pie filling, chilled

1¾ cups (4-ounce container) frozen whipped topping, thawed

Sliced almonds (optional)

BLACK FOREST TORTE

Makes 10 to 12 servings

1. Heat oven to 350°F. Grease and flour two 9-inch round baking pans.

2. Stir together sugar, flour, cocoa, baking powder, baking soda and salt in large bowl. Add eggs, milk, oil and vanilla; beat on medium speed 2 minutes. Remove from mixer; stir in boiling water (batter will be thin). Pour batter into prepared pans.

3. Bake 30 to 35 minutes or until wooden pick inserted in center comes out clean. Cool 10 minutes; remove from pans to wire rack. Cool completely.

4. Place one layer on serving plate. Spread half of pie filling over layer to within $1/2$ inch of edge. Spoon or pipe border of whipped topping around edge. Top with second cake layer. Spread remaining pie filling to within $1/2$ inch of edge. Make border around top edge with remaining topping. Garnish with sliced almonds, if desired. Refrigerate until just before serving. Cover; refrigerate leftover dessert.

½ cup (1 stick) butter or
   margarine, softened
1½ cups sugar
 2 eggs
 1 teaspoon vanilla extract
 1 cup buttermilk or sour milk*
 2 tablespoons (1-ounce
   bottle) red food color
 2 cups all-purpose flour
⅓ cup HERSHEY'S Cocoa
 1 teaspoon salt
1½ teaspoons baking soda
 1 tablespoon white vinegar
 1 can (16 ounces) ready-to-
   spread vanilla frosting
   HERSHEY'S MINI CHIPS
   Semi-Sweet Chocolate or
   HERSHEY'S Milk Chocolate
   Chips (optional)

*To sour milk: Use 1 tablespoon white
vinegar plus milk to equal 1 cup.

HERSHEY'S RED VELVET CAKE

Makes about 15 servings

1. Heat oven to 350°F. Grease and flour 13×9×2-inch baking pan.**

2. Beat butter and sugar in large bowl; add eggs and vanilla, beating well. Stir together buttermilk and food color. Stir together flour, cocoa and salt; add alternately to butter mixture with buttermilk mixture, mixing well. Stir in baking soda and vinegar. Pour into prepared pan.

3. Bake 30 to 35 minutes or until wooden pick inserted in center comes out clean. Cool completely in pan on wire rack. Frost; garnish with Mini Chips, if desired.

**This recipe can be made in 2 (9-inch) cake pans. Bake at 350°F for 30 to 35 minutes.*

Hershey's Red Velvet Cake

1 cup vanilla wafer crumbs
(about 30 wafers, crushed)

¼ cup HERSHEY'S Cocoa

¼ cup powdered sugar

¼ cup (½ stick) butter or
margarine, melted

3 packages (8 ounces each)
cream cheese, softened

1 cup granulated sugar

3 tablespoons all-purpose
flour

1 teaspoon ground pumpkin
pie spice

1 cup canned pumpkin

4 eggs

1½ cups HERSHEY'S MINI CHIPS
Semi-Sweet Chocolate

Chocolate Leaves (optional)

CHOCOLATE CHIP PUMPKIN CHEESECAKE

Makes 10 to 12 servings

1. Heat oven to 350°F. Stir together vanilla wafer crumbs, cocoa and powdered sugar in medium bowl; stir in melted butter. Press mixture onto bottom and ¹/₂ inch up side of 9-inch springform pan. Bake 8 minutes; cool slightly.

2. *Increase oven temperature to 400°F.* Beat cream cheese, granulated sugar, flour and pumpkin pie spice in large bowl until well blended. Add pumpkin and eggs; beat until well blended. Stir in Mini Chips; pour batter into prepared crust. Bake 10 minutes.

3. *Reduce oven temperature to 250°F;* continue baking 50 to 60 minutes or until almost set. Remove from oven to wire rack. With knife, loosen cake from side of pan. Cool completely. Refrigerate about 5 hours before serving. Garnish with Chocolate Leaves, if desired. Cover; refrigerate leftover cheesecake.

CHOCOLATE LEAVES: Thoroughly wash and dry several non-toxic leaves. Place ¹/₂ cup HERSHEY'S MINI CHIPS Semi-Sweet Chocolate in small microwave-safe bowl. Microwave at HIGH (100%) 30 to 45 seconds or until smooth when stirred. With small, soft-bristled pastry brush, brush melted chocolate on backs of leaves. (Avoid getting chocolate on leaf front; removal may be difficult when chocolate hardens.) Place on wax paper-covered cookie sheet; refrigerate until very firm. Beginning at stem, carefully pull green leaves from chocolate leaves; refrigerate until ready to use.

1¼ cups (2½ sticks) unsalted butter

¾ cup HERSHEY'S Cocoa

1 cup plus 1 tablespoon sugar, divided

1 tablespoon all-purpose flour

2 teaspoons vanilla extract

4 eggs, separated

1 cup (½ pint) cold whipping cream

Chocolate curls (optional)

CHOCOLATE TRUFFLE CAKE SUPREME

Makes 10 servings

1. Heat oven to 425°F. Grease bottom of 8-inch springform pan.

2. Melt butter in medium saucepan over low heat. Add cocoa and 1 cup sugar; stir well. Remove from heat; cool. Stir in flour and vanilla. Add egg yolks, one at a time, beating well after each addition. Beat egg whites in medium bowl with remaining 1 tablespoon sugar until soft peaks form; gradually fold into chocolate mixture. Spoon batter into pan.

3. Bake 16 to 18 minutes or until edge is firm (center will be soft). Cool completely on wire rack (cake will sink slightly in center as it cools). Remove side of pan. Refrigerate cake at least 6 hours.

4. Beat whipping cream in small bowl until soft peaks form; spread over top of cake. Cut cake while cold, but let stand at room temperature 10 to 15 minutes before serving. Garnish with chocolate curls, if desired.

Prep Time: 20 minutes
Bake Time: 16 minutes
Cool Time: 1 hour
Chill Time: 6 hours

15

1 cup (2 sticks) butter or
    margarine, softened

2 cups sugar

2 teaspoons vanilla extract

3 eggs

2¾ cups all-purpose flour

1¼ teaspoons baking soda,
    divided

½ teaspoon salt

1 cup buttermilk or sour milk*

1 cup HERSHEY'S Syrup

1 cup MOUNDS Sweetened
    Coconut Flakes (optional)

*To sour milk: Use 1 tablespoon white
vinegar plus milk to equal 1 cup.

CHOCOLATE SYRUP SWIRL CAKE

Makes 20 servings

1. Heat oven to 350°F. Grease and flour 12-cup fluted tube pan or 10-inch tube pan.

2. Beat butter, sugar and vanilla in large bowl until fluffy. Add eggs; beat well. Stir together flour, 1 teaspoon baking soda and salt; add alternately with buttermilk to butter mixture, beating until well blended. Measure 2 cups batter in small bowl; stir in syrup and remaining ¼ teaspoon baking soda. Add coconut, if desired, to remaining batter; pour into prepared pan. Pour chocolate batter over vanilla batter in pan; do not mix.

3. Bake 60 to 70 minutes or until wooden pick inserted in center comes out clean. Cool 15 minutes; remove from pan to wire rack. Cool completely on wire rack; glaze or frost as desired.

Chocolate Syrup Swirl Cake

1 frozen pound cake
   (10¾ ounces), thawed
½ cup powdered sugar
¼ cup HERSHEY'S Cocoa
1 cup (½ pint) cold whipping
   cream
1 teaspoon vanilla extract
   Chocolate Glaze (recipe
   follows)
   Sliced almonds (optional)

EASY CHOCOLATE CREAM-FILLED TORTE

Makes 8 to 10 servings

1. Cut cake horizontally to make 4 layers. Stir together sugar and cocoa in medium bowl. Add whipping cream and vanilla; beat until stiff.

2. Place bottom cake layer on serving platter. Spread ⅓ of the whipped cream mixture on cake layer. Place next cake layer on top of whipped cream; continue layering whipped cream mixture and cake until all has been used.

3. Prepare Chocolate Glaze; spoon over top of cake, allowing to drizzle down sides. Garnish with almonds, if desired. Refrigerate until ready to serve. Cover; refrigerate leftover torte.

Prep Time: 20 minutes
Chill Time: 30 minutes

CHOCOLATE GLAZE

Makes about ½ cup glaze

2 tablespoons butter or margarine
2 tablespoons HERSHEY'S Cocoa
2 tablespoons water
1 cup powdered sugar
¼ to ½ teaspoon almond extract

Melt butter in small saucepan over low heat. Add cocoa and water. Cook, stirring constantly, until smooth and slightly thickened. Do not boil. Remove from heat. Gradually add powdered sugar and almond extract, beating with whisk until smooth.

Easy Chocolate Cream-Filled Torte

Coconut-Pecan Graham
Crust (recipe follows)

4 bars (1 ounce each)
HERSHEY'S Semi-Sweet
Baking Chocolate, broken
into pieces

3 packages (8 ounces each)
cream cheese, softened

¾ cup sugar

½ cup dairy sour cream

2 teaspoons vanilla extract

2 tablespoons all-purpose
flour

3 eggs

Coconut-Pecan Topping
(recipe follows)

GERMAN CHOCOLATE CHEESECAKE

Makes 10 to 12 servings

1. Prepare Coconut-Pecan Graham Crust. *Increase oven temperature to 450°F.*

2. Place chocolate in small microwave-safe bowl. Microwave at HIGH (100%) 1 to 1½ minutes or until chocolate is melted and smooth when stirred. Beat cream cheese, sugar, sour cream and vanilla in large bowl on medium speed of mixer until smooth. Add flour; blend well. Add eggs and melted chocolate; beat until blended. Pour into prepared crust.

3. Bake 10 minutes. *Without opening oven door, reduce oven temperature to 250°F.* Continue baking 35 minutes. Remove from oven to wire rack. With knife, immediately loosen cake from side of pan. Cool completely; remove side of pan. Prepare Coconut-Pecan Topping; spread over cheesecake. Refrigerate several hours. Garnish as desired. Cover; refrigerate leftover cheesecake.

HERSHEY'S COCOA
AS DELICIOUS
AS HERSHEY'S
ALMOND BAR

MADE ON THE FARM

COCONUT-PECAN GRAHAM CRUST

Makes about 1¼ cups

- 1 cup graham cracker crumbs
- 2 tablespoons sugar
- ⅓ cup butter or margarine, melted
- ¼ cup MOUNDS Sweetened Coconut Flakes
- ¼ cup chopped pecans

1. Heat oven to 350°F.

2. Combine graham cracker crumbs and sugar in small bowl. Stir in butter, coconut and pecans. Press mixture onto bottom and ¹/₂ inch up side of 9-inch springform pan.

3. Bake 8 to 10 minutes or until lightly browned. Cool completely.

COCONUT-PECAN TOPPING

Makes about 1¼ cups

- ½ cup (1 stick) butter or margarine
- ¼ cup packed light brown sugar
- 2 tablespoons light cream
- 2 tablespoons light corn syrup
- 1 cup MOUNDS Sweetened Coconut Flakes
- ½ cup chopped pecans
- 1 teaspoon vanilla extract

Melt butter; add brown sugar, light cream and corn syrup in small saucepan. Cook over medium heat, stirring constantly, until smooth and bubbly. Remove from heat. Stir in coconut, pecans and vanilla. Cool slightly.

1 cup seedless black raspberry
preserves,* divided

2 cups all-purpose flour

1½ cups granulated sugar

¾ cup HERSHEY'S Cocoa

1½ teaspoons baking soda

1 teaspoon salt

⅔ cup butter or margarine,
softened

1 container (16 ounces) dairy
sour cream

2 eggs

1 teaspoon vanilla extract

Powdered sugar

Raspberry Cream (recipe
follows)

*Red raspberry jam may be substituted.

CHOCOLATE RASPBERRY POUND CAKE

Makes about 12 servings

1. Heat oven to 350°F. Grease and flour 12-cup fluted
tube pan.

2. Place ¾ cup preserves in small microwave-safe bowl.
Microwave at HIGH (100%) 30 to 45 seconds or until
melted; cool. Stir together flour, granulated sugar, cocoa,
baking soda and salt in large bowl. Add butter, sour cream,
eggs, vanilla and melted preserves; beat on medium speed
of mixer 3 to 4 minutes until well blended. Pour batter into
prepared pan.

3. Bake 50 to 60 minutes or until wooden pick inserted
in center comes out clean. Cool 10 minutes; remove from
pan to wire rack. Place remaining ¼ cup preserves in small
microwave-safe bowl. Microwave at HIGH 30 seconds or
until melted; brush over warm cake. Cool completely. Prepare
Raspberry Cream; fill cavity with cream. At serving time,
sprinkle powdered sugar over top. Garnish, if desired.

RASPBERRY CREAM: Thaw 1 package (10 ounces) frozen
red raspberries in light syrup. Purée in food processor or
blender. Strain into medium bowl; discard seeds. Blend
3½ cups (8 ounces) frozen non-dairy whipped topping,
thawed, with raspberry purée. Stir in 2 tablespoons
raspberry-flavored liqueur, if desired.

Prep Time: 35 minutes
Bake Time: 50 minutes
Cool Time: 3 hours

Chocolate Raspberry Pound Cake

Graham Cracker Crust
(recipe follows)

3 packages (8 ounces each)
cream cheese, softened

½ cup sugar

2 tablespoons all-purpose
flour

1⅔ cups (10-ounce package)
HERSHEY'S Butterscotch
Chips

2 tablespoons milk

4 eggs

Chocolate Drizzle (recipe
follows)

BUTTERSCOTCH CHEESECAKE WITH CHOCOLATE DRIZZLE

Makes 12 servings

1. Prepare Graham Cracker Crust. *Increase oven temperature to 350°F.*

2. Beat cream cheese, sugar and flour in large bowl on medium speed of mixer until smooth. Place butterscotch chips and milk in small microwave-safe bowl. Microwave at HIGH (100%) 1 minute; stir. If necessary, microwave at HIGH an additional 15 seconds at a time, stirring after each heating, just until chips are melted when stirred.

3. Blend butterscotch mixture into cream cheese mixture. Add eggs, one at a time, blending well after each addition. Pour mixture over prepared crust.

4. Bake 40 to 45 minutes or until almost set in center. Remove from oven to wire rack. With knife, immediately loosen cake from side of pan. Cool completely; remove side of pan.

5. Prepare Chocolate Drizzle; drizzle over cheesecake. Refrigerate leftover cheesecake.

GRAHAM CRACKER CRUST

1 cup graham cracker crumbs

3 tablespoons sugar

3 tablespoons butter or margarine, melted

Heat oven to 325°F. Stir together crumbs, sugar and butter in small bowl. Press mixture onto bottom of 9-inch springform pan. Bake 10 minutes. Cool completely.

CHOCOLATE DRIZZLE

½ cup HERSHEY'S Semi-Sweet Chocolate Chips

1 tablespoon shortening (do not use butter, margarine, spread or oil)

Place chocolate chips and shortening in small microwave-safe bowl. Microwave at HIGH (100%) 30 seconds; stir. If necessary, microwave at HIGH an additional 15 seconds at a time, stirring after each heating, just until chips are melted when stirred.

HERSHEY'S HINT

Cheesecakes are generally baked in special two-piece springform pans. As the name implies, there is a spring or clamp on the side of the pan that opens, allowing for easy removal of the cheesecake from the pan.

6 eggs

1 cup sugar

1 teaspoon vanilla extract

½ cup all-purpose flour

½ cup HERSHEY'S Cocoa

½ cup (1 stick) butter or margarine, melted and cooled slightly

Peanut Butter Cream Filling (page 28)

8 tablespoons apricot preserves, strained and divided

Fresh fruit slices (optional)

Elegant Chocolate Torte

Makes 10 to 12 servings

1. Heat oven to 350°F. Grease and flour three 8-inch round baking pans.

2. Beat eggs in large bowl until foamy; gradually add sugar, beating until thick and lemon colored, about 5 minutes. Stir in vanilla. Stir together flour and cocoa; with rubber spatula, gradually fold into egg mixture. Fold in butter until well blended. Divide batter evenly among prepared pans.

3. Bake 15 minutes or until top springs back when touched lightly. Cool 5 minutes; remove from pans to wire racks. Cool completely. Meanwhile, prepare Peanut Butter Cream Filling.

4. Spread top surface of each cake layer with 2 tablespoons apricot preserves. Place one cake layer, apricot-side-up, on serving plate. Spread one-third of the filling over preserves. Set second layer, apricot-side-up, on top of first layer; spread with one-third of filling. Top with third cake layer; spread with remaining filling. Spread remaining 2 tablespoons apricot preserves on top. Cover; refrigerate until just before serving. Garnish with fresh fruit, if desired.

NOTE: Torte will stack best if each layer is spread with filling and refrigerated until set before assembling.

continued on page 28

Elegant Chocolate Torte

Elegant Chocolate Torte, continued

PEANUT BUTTER CREAM FILLING

Makes about 3 cups filling

- 1½ cups miniature marshmallows
- 1 cup REESE'S Peanut Butter Chips
- ⅓ cup milk
- 1 cup (½ pint) cold whipping cream
- ½ teaspoon vanilla extract

1. Place marshmallows and peanut butter chips in milk in small microwave-safe bowl. Microwave at HIGH (100%) 1 minute; stir. If necessary, microwave an additional 15 seconds at a time, stirring after each heating, until mixture is smooth when stirred. Cool to lukewarm.

2. Beat whipping cream in medium bowl until stiff; fold in vanilla and peanut butter mixture. If filling is too soft to spread, refrigerate for a short time.

HERSHEY'S HINT

Never substitute cocoa mixes, which contain sugars and other flavorings, for unsweetened cocoa powder. For maximum freshness, store cocoa powder sealed in an airtight container in a cool, dry place.

Chocolate Wafer Crust
(recipe follows)

1⅔ cups (10-ounce package)
HERSHEY'S Raspberry
Chips

2 packages (8 ounces each)
cream cheese, softened

¾ cup sugar

4 eggs

1 container (8 ounces) sour
cream

1 teaspoon vanilla extract

Sweetened whipped cream

Fresh raspberries (optional)

CHOCOLATE RASPBERRY CHEESECAKE
Makes 10 to 12 servings

1. Prepare Chocolate Wafer Crust. Heat oven to 325°F. Place chips in medium microwave-safe bowl. Microwave at HIGH (100%) 1 minute; stir. If necessary, microwave at HIGH an additional 15 seconds at a time, stirring after each heating, just until chips are melted when stirred.

2. Beat cream cheese and sugar in large bowl on medium speed of mixer until smooth. Blend in melted chips. Add eggs, one at a time, beating well after each addition. Add sour cream and vanilla; blend well. Pour into prepared crust.

3. Bake 55 to 60 minutes or until almost set in center. Remove from oven to wire rack. Immediately loosen edge of cake from side of pan with knife. Cool completely.

4. Remove side of pan; cover and refrigerate several hours. Just before serving, garnish with sweetened whipped cream and raspberries, if desired. Refrigerate leftover cheesecake.

CHOCOLATE WAFER CRUST

6 tablespoons butter or margarine
1½ cups vanilla wafer crumbs (about 45 wafers)
6 tablespoons powdered sugar
6 tablespoons HERSHEY'S Cocoa

Place butter in medium microwave-safe bowl. Microwave at HIGH (100%) 30 seconds or until melted. Stir in crumbs, powdered sugar and cocoa; blend well. Press mixture onto bottom and ½ inch up side of 9-inch springform pan.

1 cup water

1 cup (2 sticks) butter or margarine

½ cup HERSHEY'S Cocoa

2 cups sugar

1¾ cups all-purpose flour

1 teaspoon baking soda

½ teaspoon salt

3 eggs

¾ cup dairy sour cream

Peanut Butter Chip Frosting (recipe follows)

Chocolate Garnish (optional, recipe follows)

TAKE-ME-TO-A-PICNIC CAKE

Makes about 20 servings

1. Heat oven to 350°F. Grease and flour $15\frac{1}{2}\times10\frac{1}{2}\times1$-inch jelly-roll pan.

2. Combine water, butter and cocoa in medium saucepan. Cook over medium heat, stirring occasionally, until mixture boils. Boil 1 minute. Remove from heat. Stir together sugar, flour, baking soda and salt in large bowl. Add eggs and sour cream; beat until blended. Add cocoa mixture; beat just until blended. Pour into prepared pan.

3. Bake 25 to 30 minutes or until wooden pick inserted in center comes out clean. Cool on wire rack. Prepare Peanut Butter Chip Frosting. Spread over cake. Prepare Chocolate Garnish; drizzle over top, if desired.

PEANUT BUTTER CHIP FROSTING: Combine $\frac{1}{3}$ cup butter or margarine, $\frac{1}{3}$ cup milk and $1\frac{2}{3}$ cups (10-ounce package) REESE'S Peanut Butter Chips in medium saucepan. Cook over low heat, stirring constantly, until chips are melted and mixture is smooth. Remove from heat; stir in 1 teaspoon vanilla extract. Place 1 cup powdered sugar in medium bowl. Gradually add chip mixture; beat well. Makes about 2 cups frosting.

CHOCOLATE GARNISH: Place $\frac{1}{2}$ cup HERSHEY'S Semi-Sweet Chocolate Chips and 1 teaspoon shortening (not butter, margarine, spread or oil) in small microwave-safe bowl. Microwave at HIGH (100%) 1 minute; stir until chips are melted and mixture is smooth.

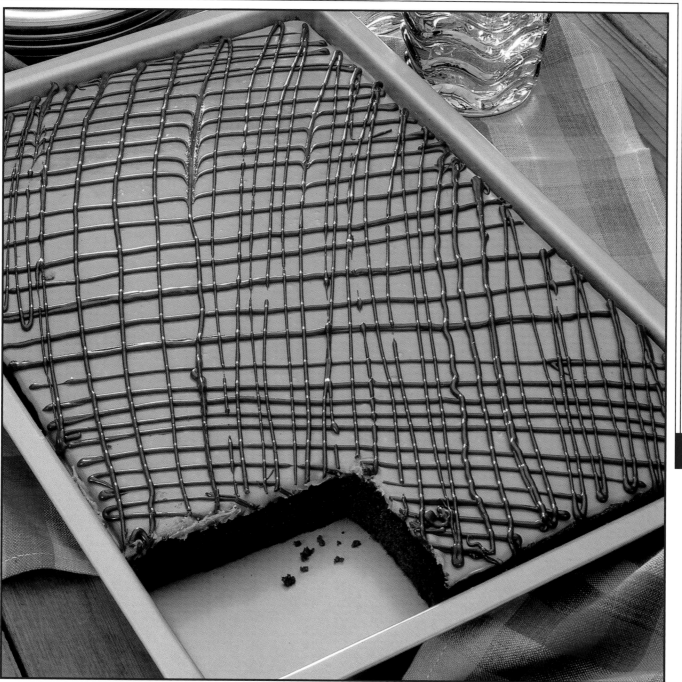

Take-Me-To-A-Picnic Cake

¼ cup HERSHEY'S Cocoa

½ cup boiling water

1 cup plus 3 tablespoons
   butter or margarine,
   softened

2¼ cups sugar

1 teaspoon vanilla extract

4 eggs

2 cups all-purpose flour

1 teaspoon baking soda

½ teaspoon salt

1 cup buttermilk or sour milk*

Coconut Pecan Frosting
   (recipe follows)

Pecan halves (optional)

*To sour milk: Use 1 tablespoon white
vinegar plus milk to equal 1 cup.

GERMAN CHOCOLATE CAKE

Makes 10 to 12 servings

1. Heat oven to 350°F. Grease and flour three 9-inch round baking pans. Combine cocoa and water in small bowl; stir until smooth. Set aside to cool.

2. Beat butter, sugar and vanilla in large bowl until fluffy. Add eggs, one at a time, beating well after each addition. Stir together flour, baking soda and salt; add alternately with chocolate mixture and buttermilk to butter mixture. Mix only until smooth. Pour batter into prepared pans.

3. Bake 25 to 30 minutes or until top springs back when touched lightly. Cool 5 minutes; remove from pans. Cool completely on wire rack. Prepare Coconut Pecan Frosting; spread between layers and over top. Garnish with pecan halves, if desired.

COCONUT PECAN FROSTING

Makes about 2²/₃ cups frosting

1 can (14 ounces) sweetened condensed milk

½ cup butter or margarine

3 egg yolks, slightly beaten

1 teaspoon vanilla extract

1⅓ cups MOUNDS Sweetened Coconut Flakes

1 cup chopped pecans

Place sweetened condensed milk, butter and egg yolks in saucepan. Cook over low heat, stirring constantly, until mixture is thickened and bubbly. Remove from heat; stir in vanilla, coconut and pecans. Cool to room temperature.

German Chocolate Cake

⅓ cup butter or margarine, melted

1 ¼ cups graham cracker crumbs

⅓ cup HERSHEY'S Cocoa

⅓ cup sugar

1 cup REESE'S Peanut Butter Chips

2 packages (8 ounces each) cream cheese, softened

1 can (14 ounces) sweetened condensed milk (not evaporated milk)

4 eggs

1 teaspoon vanilla extract

Sweetened whipped cream and chocolate curls or shavings (optional)

PEANUT BUTTER CHIP CHEESECAKE

Makes 12 servings

1. Heat oven to 300°F.

2. Stir together butter, graham cracker crumbs, cocoa and sugar in medium bowl; press firmly onto bottom of 9-inch springform pan or 13×9-inch baking pan.

3. Place peanut butter chips in small microwave-safe bowl. Microwave at HIGH (100%) 1 minute; stir. If necessary, microwave at HIGH an additional 15 seconds at a time, stirring after each heating, just until chips are melted when stirred. Meanwhile, beat cream cheese until fluffy. Gradually beat in sweetened condensed milk and melted chips until smooth. Add eggs and vanilla; mix well. Pour into prepared crust.

4. Bake 50 to 60 minutes or until cheesecake springs back when lightly touched. Cool to room temperature. Refrigerate. Garnish with sweetened whipped cream, chocolate curls or shavings, if desired. Cover; refrigerate leftover cheesecake.

Prep Time: 30 minutes
Bake Time: 50 minutes
Cool Time: 1 hour
Chill Time: 4 hours

Chocolate Cookie Crust
(recipe follows)

4 packages (3 ounces each)
cream cheese, softened

3 tablespoons butter or
margarine, softened

1 cup sugar

⅓ cup HERSHEY'S Cocoa

1½ teaspoons vanilla extract

2 eggs

1 container (8 ounces) dairy
sour cream

Sweetened whipped cream
(optional)

COCOA CHEESECAKE SUPREME

Makes 10 to 12 servings

1. Prepare Chocolate Cookie Crust; set aside.

2. Heat oven to 325°F. Beat cream cheese and butter in large bowl until smooth; gradually beat in sugar. Beat in cocoa and vanilla until well blended. Add eggs, one at a time, beating well after each addition. Add sour cream; blend well. Pour batter into prepared crust.

3. Bake 30 minutes. Turn off oven; leave cheesecake in oven 15 minutes without opening oven door. Remove from oven. Loosen cheesecake from side of pan; cool to room temperature. Refrigerate several hours or overnight; remove side of pan. Garnish with sweetened whipped cream, if desired. Cover; refrigerate leftover cheesecake.

CHOCOLATE COOKIE CRUST: Crush 22 chocolate wafers (one-half of 8½-ounce package) in food processor or blender to form fine crumbs (1 cup). Cut ¼ cup cold butter or margarine into ½-inch pieces. Mix crumbs, butter pieces and ⅛ teaspoon ground cinnamon in medium bowl until evenly blended. Press mixture onto bottom of 9-inch springform pan.

35

1 cup sugar, divided

½ cup (1 stick) butter or
   margarine, softened

1 egg

2 teaspoons vanilla extract,
   divided

1½ cups all-purpose flour

½ teaspoon baking powder

1 cup HERSHEY'S MINI CHIPS
   Semi-Sweet Chocolate *or*
   HERSHEY'S Semi-Sweet
   Chocolate Chips, divided

2 cups dairy sour cream

2 eggs

2 cups frozen non-dairy
   whipped topping, thawed

Fresh strawberries, rinsed
   and halved

STRAWBERRY CHOCOLATE CHIP SHORTCAKE

Makes 12 servings

1. Heat oven to 350°F. Grease 9-inch springform pan.

2. Beat $1/2$ cup sugar and butter in large bowl. Add 1 egg and 1 teaspoon vanilla; beat until creamy. Gradually add flour and baking powder, beating until smooth; stir in $1/2$ cup Mini Chips. Press mixture onto bottom of prepared pan.

3. Stir together sour cream, remaining $1/2$ cup sugar, 2 eggs and remaining 1 teaspoon vanilla in medium bowl; stir in remaining $1/2$ cup Mini Chips. Pour over mixture in pan.

4. Bake 50 to 55 minutes or until almost set in center and edges are lightly browned. Cool completely on wire rack; remove side of pan. Spread whipped topping over top. Cover; refrigerate. Just before serving, arrange strawberry halves on top of cake; garnish as desired. Refrigerate leftover dessert.

37

Strawberry Chocolate Chip Shortcake

½ cup HERSHEY'S Cocoa *or* HERSHEY'S Dutch Processed Cocoa

½ cup boiling water

⅔ cup shortening

1¾ cups sugar

1 teaspoon vanilla extract

2 eggs

2¼ cups all-purpose flour

1½ teaspoons baking soda

½ teaspoon salt

1⅓ cups buttermilk or sour milk*

One-Bowl Buttercream Frosting (recipe follows)

To sour milk: Use 4 teaspoons white vinegar plus milk to equal 1⅓ cups.

CHOCOLATETOWN SPECIAL CAKE

Makes 8 to 10 servings

1. Heat oven to 350°F. Grease and flour two 9-inch round baking pans.

2. Stir together cocoa and water in small bowl until smooth. Beat shortening, sugar and vanilla in large bowl until fluffy. Add eggs; beat well. Stir together flour, baking soda and salt; add to shortening mixture alternately with buttermilk, beating until well blended. Add cocoa mixture; beat well. Pour batter into prepared pans.

3. Bake 35 to 40 minutes or until wooden pick inserted in center comes out clean. Cool 10 minutes; remove from pans to wire racks. Cool completely. Prepare One-Bowl Buttercream Frosting; spread between layers and over top and sides of cake.

ONE-BOWL BUTTERCREAM FROSTING

Makes about 2 cups frosting

6 tablespoons butter *or* margarine, softened

2⅔ cups powdered sugar

½ cup HERSHEY'S Cocoa or HERSHEY'S Dutch Processed Cocoa

4 to 6 tablespoons milk

1 teaspoon vanilla extract

Beat butter in medium bowl. Add powdered sugar and cocoa alternately with milk, beating to spreading consistency. Stir in vanilla.

43

Chocolate Golf Course Cake

Chocolate Golf Course Cake, continued

GRASS AND GREENS FROSTING

Makes about 2½ cups

> ½ cup (1 stick) butter or margarine, softened
> 1 pound (about 4 cups) powdered sugar, divided
> 3 to 4 tablespoons milk
> 1 teaspoon vanilla extract

1. Beat butter until creamy in large bowl. Gradually add about one-half of the powdered sugar, beating well. Slowly beat in milk and vanilla.

2. Gradually add remaining powdered sugar, beating until smooth. Add additional milk, if necessary, until desired spreading consistency.

H E R S H E Y ' S   H I N T

Show Dad how much you care and make Father's Day extra special. He will surely be delighted with this delicious and fun-to-make cake.

2 packages (about 15 ounces each) nut quick bread mix

1½ cups sugar

½ cup HERSHEY'S Cocoa

1 teaspoon ground cinnamon

1½ cups vegetable oil

6 eggs

3 cups shredded zucchini

Chocolate Buttercream Frosting (recipe follows)

EASY HARVEST CHOCOLATE CAKE

Makes 12 servings

1. Heat oven to 350°F. Grease and flour three 8-inch round baking pans.

2. Stir together bread mix, sugar, cocoa, cinnamon, oil and eggs in large bowl until well blended. Stir in zucchini; pour evenly into prepared pans.

3. Bake 40 to 45 minutes or until wooden pick inserted in center comes out clean. Cool 10 minutes; remove from pans to wire rack. Cool completely. Prepare Chocolate Buttercream Frosting; spread between layers and over top and side of cake.

CHOCOLATE BUTTERCREAM FROSTING: Stir together 5⅓ cups powdered sugar and ½ cup HERSHEY'S Cocoa in large bowl. In another large bowl, beat ¾ cup (1½ sticks) softened butter and about 1 cup sugar-cocoa mixture. Add remaining sugar-cocoa mixture, ½ cup milk and 2 teaspoons vanilla extract; beat to spreading consistency.

45

1 ¼ cups graham cracker crumbs

⅓ cup plus ¼ cup sugar, divided

⅓ cup HERSHEY'S Cocoa

⅓ cup butter or margarine, melted

3 packages (8 ounces each) cream cheese, softened

1 can (14 ounces) sweetened condensed milk (not evaporated milk)

1 ⅔ cups (10-ounce package) REESE'S Peanut Butter Chips, melted

4 eggs

2 teaspoons vanilla extract

Chocolate Drizzle (recipe follows)

Whipped topping

HERSHEY'S MINI KISSES Semi-Sweet *or* Milk Chocolate Baking Pieces

REESE'S CHOCOLATE PEANUT BUTTER CHEESECAKE

Makes 12 servings

1. Heat oven to 300°F. Combine graham cracker crumbs, $^1/_3$ cup sugar, cocoa and butter; press onto bottom of 9-inch springform pan.

2. Beat cream cheese and remaining $^1/_4$ cup sugar until fluffy. Gradually beat in sweetened condensed milk, then melted chips, until smooth. Add eggs and vanilla; beat well. Pour into prepared crust.

3. Bake 60 to 70 minutes or until center is almost set. Remove from oven. With knife, loosen cake from side of pan. Cool. Remove side of pan. Refrigerate until cold. Garnish with Chocolate Drizzle, whipped topping and Mini Kisses. Store, covered, in refrigerator.

CHOCOLATE DRIZZLE: Melt 2 tablespoons butter in small saucepan over low heat; add 2 tablespoons HERSHEY'S Cocoa and 2 tablespoons water. Cook and stir until slightly thickened. Do not boil. Cool slightly. Gradually add 1 cup powdered sugar and $^1/_2$ teaspoon vanilla extract, beating with whisk until smooth. Makes about $^3/_4$ cup.

TIP: If desired, spoon drizzle into small heavy seal-top plastic bag. With scissors, make small diagonal cut in bottom corner of bag. Squeeze drizzle over top of cake.

Reese's Chocolate Peanut Butter Cheesecake

2 cups all-purpose flour

1½ cups sugar

⅔ cup HERSHEY'S Cocoa

2 teaspoons baking powder

½ teaspoon baking soda

½ teaspoon salt

⅔ cup shortening

2 eggs

⅔ cup milk

½ cup hot water

1½ teaspoons vanilla extract

Creamy Fudge Frosting
(recipe follows)

QUICK 'N' EASY CHOCOLATE CUPCAKES

Makes about 30 cupcakes

1. Heat oven to 350°F. Line muffin cups (2½ inches in diameter) with paper bake cups.

2. Stir together flour, sugar, cocoa, baking powder, baking soda and salt in large bowl. Add shortening, eggs, milk, water and vanilla; beat on low speed of mixer 1 minute. Beat on medium speed an additional 3 minutes or until mixture is smooth. Fill cups ½ full with batter.

3. Bake 15 to 20 minutes or until center of cupcake springs back when touched lightly in center. Remove cupcakes from pan to wire rack. Cool completely. (Do not cool cupcakes in pan; paper liners will come loose from cupcakes.)

4. Prepare Creamy Fudge Frosting; frost cupcakes. Decorate, if desired.

Prep Time: 45 minutes
Bake Time: 15 minutes
Cool Time: 1 hour

CREAMY FUDGE FROSTING

Makes about 2 cups frosting

½ cup (1 stick) butter or margarine

½ cup HERSHEY'S Cocoa

3⅔ cups (1 pound) powdered sugar

1½ teaspoons vanilla extract

Dash salt

⅓ cup water

Melt butter in medium saucepan over low heat. Add cocoa; stir until smooth and well blended. Remove from heat. Add powdered sugar, vanilla and salt alternately with water; beat with spoon or whisk until smooth and creamy. Additional water may be added, $^1/_2$ teaspoon at a time, if frosting becomes too thick.

HERSHEY'S HINT

Butter, margarine and cream cheese will blend better with other ingredients in the recipe if removed from the refrigerator and allowed to soften and come to room temperature first.

2/3 cup butter or margarine, softened

1 3/4 cups sugar

2 eggs

1 1/4 teaspoons almond extract

1 teaspoon vanilla extract

1 3/4 cups all-purpose flour

3/4 cup HERSHEY'S Dutch Processed Cocoa

1 1/2 teaspoons baking soda

1 1/2 cups dairy sour cream

Powdered sugar

Cherry Whipped Cream (recipe follows)

Maraschino cherries (optional)

FLUTED CHOCOLATE-MARASCHINO CAKE

Makes 12 servings

1. Heat oven to 350°F. Grease and flour 12-cup fluted tube pan.

2. Beat butter and sugar in large bowl until creamy. Add eggs and almond and vanilla extracts; beat well. Combine flour, cocoa and baking soda; add to butter mixture alternately with sour cream, beating well. Pour into prepared pan.

3. Bake 45 to 50 minutes or until wooden pick inserted in center comes out clean. Cool 15 minutes; remove from pan to wire rack. Cool completely. Sift with powdered sugar. Garnish with Cherry Whipped Cream and maraschino cherries, if desired.

CHERRY WHIPPED CREAM: Beat 1 cup (1/2 pint) cold whipping cream, 3 tablespoons powdered sugar, 1/2 teaspoon almond extract and 1/4 teaspoon vanilla extract in medium bowl until stiff. Stir in 1/2 cup chopped maraschino cherries. Makes about 1 cup.

Fluted Chocolate-Maraschino Cake

Almond Crumb Crust
(recipe follows)

1 package (8 ounces)
HERSHEY'S Semi-Sweet
Baking Chocolate, broken
into pieces

3 packages (3 ounces each)
cream cheese, softened

¼ cup sugar

¼ cup (½ stick) butter or
margarine, softened

1 teaspoon vanilla extract

1 cup (½ pint) cold whipping
cream

52

EASY RICH NO-BAKE CHOCOLATE CHEESECAKE

Makes about 8 servings

1. Prepare Almond Crumb Crust; set aside.

2. Place chocolate in small microwave-safe bowl. Microwave at HIGH (100%) 1 to 1½ minutes or until chocolate is melted when stirred. Set aside; cool slightly. Beat cream cheese, sugar, butter and vanilla in large bowl until smooth. Add melted chocolate; beat on low speed of mixer.

3. Beat whipping cream in small bowl until stiff; fold into chocolate mixture. Pour mixture into prepared crust. Cover; refrigerate until firm.

ALMOND CRUMB CRUST: Heat oven to 350°F. Stir together 1 cup finely chopped slivered almonds, ³/₄ cup vanilla wafer crumbs and ¹/₄ cup powdered sugar in medium bowl. Pour ¹/₄ cup (¹/₂ stick) melted butter or margarine over crumb mixture; blend well. Press mixture onto bottom and ¹/₂ inch up side of 9-inch springform pan. Bake 8 to 10 minutes or until lightly browned. Cool completely.

Prep Time: 25 minutes
Bake Time: 8 minutes
Chill Time: 4 hours

Almond Graham Crust
(recipe follows)

1 HERSHEY'S SYMPHONY Milk
Chocolate Bar *or* Milk
Chocolate Bar With
Almonds & Toffee Chips
(7 ounces), broken into
pieces

4 packages (3 ounces each)
cream cheese, softened

½ cup sugar

2 tablespoons HERSHEY'S
Cocoa

⅛ teaspoon salt

2 eggs

1 teaspoon vanilla extract
Sweetened whipped cream
(optional)

GRAND FINALE CHEESECAKE

Makes 8 servings

1. Prepare Almond Graham Crust. Heat oven to 325°F.

2. Place chocolate in small microwave-safe bowl. Microwave at HIGH (100%) 1 minute or until chocolate is melted and smooth when stirred. In large bowl, beat cream cheese until smooth. Stir together sugar, cocoa and salt; blend into cream cheese mixture. Add eggs and vanilla; beat until well blended. Add melted chocolate; beat just until blended. Pour into prepared crust.

3. Bake 35 to 40 minutes or until set in center. Remove from oven to wire rack. With knife, immediately loosen cake from side of pan. Cool completely; remove side of pan. Refrigerate several hours before serving. Garnish with sweetened whipped cream, if desired. Cover; refrigerate leftover cheesecake.

ALMOND GRAHAM CRUST

    ¾ cup graham cracker crumbs
    ⅔ cup finely chopped slivered almonds
    2 tablespoons sugar
    ¼ cup (½ stick) butter or margarine, melted

Stir together graham cracker crumbs, almonds and sugar in medium bowl. Stir in butter. Press mixture onto bottom and up side of 8-inch springform pan.

1 ½ cups all-purpose flour

1 cup sugar

¼ cup HERSHEY'S Cocoa

1 teaspoon baking soda

½ teaspoon salt

1 cup water

¼ cup plus 2 tablespoons vegetable oil

1 tablespoon white vinegar

1 teaspoon vanilla extract

Broiled Topping (recipe follows)

CRUNCHY-TOPPED COCOA CAKE

Makes 9 servings

1. Heat oven to 350°F. Grease and flour 8-inch square baking pan.

2. Stir together flour, sugar, cocoa, baking soda and salt in large bowl. Add water, oil, vinegar and vanilla; beat with spoon or whisk just until batter is smooth and ingredients are well blended. Pour batter into prepared pan.

3. Bake 35 to 40 minutes or until wooden pick inserted in center comes out clean. Meanwhile, prepare Broiled Topping; spread on warm cake. Set oven to broil; place pan about 4 inches from heat. Broil 3 minutes or until top is bubbly and golden brown. Remove from oven. Cool completely in pan on wire rack.

BROILED TOPPING

Makes about 1 cup topping

¼ cup (½ stick) butter or margarine, softened

½ cup packed light brown sugar

½ cup coarsely chopped nuts

½ cup MOUNDS Sweetened Coconut Flakes

3 tablespoons light cream or evaporated milk

Stir together all ingredients in small bowl until well blended.

Prep Time: 20 minutes
Bake Time: 35 minutes
Cool Time: 1½ hours

Crunchy-Topped Cocoa Cake

Orange Cream (recipe follows)

6 eggs, separated

1⅔ cups plus 1 tablespoon
sugar, divided

1 cup all-purpose flour

⅔ cup HERSHEY'S Cocoa

1 teaspoon baking soda

⅔ cup water

Chocolate Cream Frosting
(recipe follows)

Sweetened whipped cream
or grated orange peel
(optional)

PINWHEEL CHOCOLATE CAKE

Makes 12 to 14 servings

1. Heat oven to 375°F. Line 15½×10½×1-inch jelly-roll pan with foil; generously grease foil.

2. Prepare Orange Cream; set aside. Beat egg yolks on high speed of mixer in large bowl until thick and lemon colored, about 3 minutes. Gradually add 1 cup sugar; beat 2 minutes. Stir together flour, cocoa, ⅔ cup sugar and baking soda. Add alternately with water to egg yolk mixture; beat on low speed until smooth. Beat egg whites in large bowl until foamy. Add 1 tablespoon sugar; beat until stiff peaks form. Fold into chocolate mixture. Pour 3 cups batter into prepared pan (set aside remaining batter).

3. Bake 15 to 18 minutes or until top springs back when touched lightly in center. Invert onto clean towel sprinkled with powdered sugar; cool completely. Repeat baking procedure with remaining batter.

4. Cut each cake into five rectangles, about 2¾ inches wide. Spread slightly heaping ⅓ cup Orange Cream over each rectangle to ends. Beginning with one short end, roll up one of the strips, jelly-roll fashion; place, cut side up, in center of 9-inch springform pan. Wrap remaining strips tightly around center roll, forming a large spiral to fill pan. If necessary, loosen sides of pan to fit last few pieces. Cover; refrigerate 1 hour or until cream is firm. Remove sides of pan.

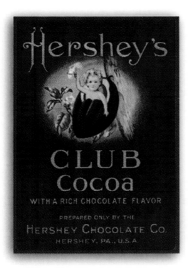

5. Prepare Chocolate Cream Frosting; frost cake. Garnish with sweetened whipped cream or orange peel, if desired. Refrigerate at least 3 hours before serving. Cover; refrigerate leftover cake.

ORANGE CREAM: Combine 2 packages (4-serving size each) vanilla instant pudding and pie filling, 3 cups milk, 2 tablespoons Grand Marnier (orange-flavored liqueur) or $1/2$ teaspoon orange extract and a few drops red food color in large bowl. Beat with whisk until thickened.

CHOCOLATE CREAM FROSTING: Combine $2/3$ cup sugar and $1/3$ cup HERSHEY'S Cocoa in large bowl. Add $11/4$ cups cold whipping cream and 1 teaspoon vanilla extract; beat until stiff. Makes about $21/2$ cups.

Prep Time: 45 minutes
Bake Time: 30 minutes
Cool Time: 1 hour
Chill Time: 4 hours

57

HERSHEY'S HINT

Unsweetened cocoa is formed by extracting most of the cocoa butter from pure chocolate and grinding the remaining chocolate solids into a powder.

½ cup (1 stick) butter or margarine, softened

¾ cup sugar

⅓ cup REESE'S Creamy *or* Crunchy Peanut Butter

1 egg

½ teaspoon vanilla extract

1 ¼ cups all-purpose flour

½ teaspoon baking soda

¼ teaspoon salt

16 REESE'S Peanut Butter Cup Miniatures, cut into fourths

GIANT PEANUT BUTTER CUP COOKIES

Makes 9 cookies

1. Heat oven to 350°F.

2. Beat butter, sugar and peanut butter in medium bowl until creamy. Add egg and vanilla; beat well. Stir together flour, baking soda and salt. Add to butter mixture; blend well. Drop dough by level $1/4$-cup measurements onto ungreased cookie sheets, three cookies per sheet. (Cookies will spread while baking.) Push about seven pieces of peanut butter cup into each cookie, flattening cookie slightly.

3. Bake 15 to 17 minutes or until light golden brown around the edges. Centers will be pale and slightly soft. Cool 1 minute on cookie sheet. Remove to wire racks; cool completely.

59

Giant Peanut Butter Cup Cookies

½ cup (1 stick) butter or
    margarine, softened

1¼ cups sugar

2 eggs

1 teaspoon almond extract

2¼ cups all-purpose flour

¼ cup HERSHEY'S Dutch
    Processed Cocoa *or*
    HERSHEY'S Cocoa

1 teaspoon baking powder

¼ teaspoon salt

1 cup sliced almonds

    Chocolate Glaze (recipe
    follows)

    White Glaze (page 62)

    Additional sliced almonds
    (optional)

CHOCOLATE ALMOND BISCOTTI

Makes about 2½ dozen cookies

1. Heat oven to 350°F. Beat butter and sugar until blended. Add eggs and almond extract; beat well. Stir together flour, cocoa, baking powder and salt; gradually add to butter mixture, beating until smooth. (Dough will be thick.) Stir in almonds using wooden spoon.

2. Shape dough into two 11-inch-long rolls. Place rolls 3 to 4 inches apart on large ungreased cookie sheet.

3. Bake 30 minutes or until rolls are set. Remove from oven; cool on cookie sheet 15 minutes. Using serrated knife, cut rolls diagonally using sawing motion, into ½-inch-thick slices. Arrange slices, cut sides down, close together on cookie sheet.

4. Bake 8 to 9 minutes. Turn slices over; bake an additional 8 to 9 minutes. Remove from oven; cool on cookie sheet on wire rack. Prepare Chocolate Glaze. Dip end of each biscotti in glaze or drizzle over entire cookie. Prepare White Glaze; drizzle over chocolate glaze. Garnish with additional almonds, if desired.

CHOCOLATE GLAZE: Place 1 cup HERSHEY'S Semi-Sweet Chocolate Chips and 1 tablespoon shortening (do not use butter, margarine, spread or oil) into small microwave-safe bowl. Microwave at HIGH (100%) 1 to 1½ minutes or until smooth when stirred. Makes about 1 cup glaze.

continued on page 62

Chocolate Almond Biscotti

Chocolate Almond Biscotti, continued

WHITE GLAZE: Place ¹/₄ cup HERSHEY'S Premier White Chips and 1 teaspoon shortening (do not use butter, margarine, spread or oil) into small microwave-safe bowl. Microwave at HIGH (100%) 30 to 45 seconds or until smooth when stirred. Makes about ¹/₄ cup glaze.

Prep Time: 30 minutes
Bake Time: 46 minutes
Cool Time: 1 hour

HERSHEY'S HINT

Hershey's Dutch Processed Cocoa is unsweetened cocoa that is treated with an alkali. It has a dark reddish color and provides a unique rich flavor for everything from hot cocoa to special chocolate desserts.

½ cup shortening

¾ cup REESE'S Creamy Peanut Butter

1¼ cups packed light brown sugar

3 tablespoons milk

1 tablespoon vanilla extract

1 egg

1½ cups all-purpose flour

¾ teaspoon baking soda

¾ teaspoon salt

1⅓ cups (8-ounce package) HEATH BITS, divided

HEATH BITS PEANUT BUTTER COOKIES

Makes about 3 dozen cookies

1. Heat oven to 375°F.

2. Beat shortening, peanut butter, brown sugar, milk and vanilla in large bowl until well blended. Add egg; beat just until blended. Combine flour, baking soda and salt; gradually beat into peanut butter mixture. Stir in 1 cup Heath Bits; reserve remainder for topping.

3. Drop by heaping teaspoons about 2 inches apart onto ungreased cookie sheet; top each with reserved Heath Bits.

4. Bake 7 to 8 minutes or until set. Do not overbake. Cool 2 minutes. Remove to wire racks. Cool completely.

¼ cup Candied Orange Peel
(page 66)

½ cup (1 stick) butter
(no substitutes)

⅔ cup sugar

2 tablespoons milk

2 tablespoons light corn syrup

⅓ cup all-purpose flour

1 cup sliced almonds

1 teaspoon vanilla extract

Chocolate Filling
(page 66)

CHOCOLATE FLORENTINES
Makes about 1½ dozen filled cookies

1. Prepare Candied Orange Peel.

2. Heat oven to 350°F. Line cookie sheets with heavy-duty foil; smooth out wrinkles.

3. Place butter, sugar, milk and corn syrup in medium saucepan. Cook over medium heat, stirring constantly, until mixture boils. Continue cooking, without stirring, until syrup reaches 230°F on candy thermometer or until syrup spins 2-inch thread when dropped from fork or spoon. Remove from heat. Stir in flour, Candied Orange Peel, almonds and vanilla. (To keep mixture from hardening, immediately place pan over hot water.) Drop mixture by level teaspoons onto prepared cookie sheets, placing at least 4 inches apart. (Cookies will spread a great deal during baking.)

4. Bake 8 to 11 minutes or until cookies are bubbly all over and are light brown caramel color. Remove from oven; cool. (Carefully slide foil off cookie sheet to reuse cookie sheet; prepare with foil for next use.) Cool cookies completely on foil; gently peel off foil.

5. Prepare Chocolate Filling; spread thin layer on flat side of one cookie; gently press on another cookie, flat sides together. Wrap individually in plastic wrap. Repeat with remaining cookies and filling. Store tightly covered in refrigerator. *continued on page 66*

65

Chocolate Florentines

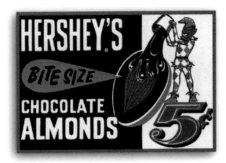

Chocolate Florentines, continued

CANDIED ORANGE PEEL: Cut outer peel (no white membrane) of 2 small navel oranges into $1/2$-inch-wide strips. Cut across strips to make $1/2 \times 1/8$-inch pieces. In small saucepan, place peel, $1/4$ cup sugar and $1/2$ cup water. Cook over very low heat until bottom of pan is covered only with glazed peel; do not caramelize. Remove from heat; spoon onto wax paper. Cool.

CHOCOLATE FILLING: In small microwave-safe bowl, place 1 cup HERSHEY'S Semi-Sweet Chocolate Chips. Microwave at HIGH (100%) 1 minute; stir. If necessary, microwave at HIGH an additional 15 seconds at a time, stirring after each heating, just until chips are melted when stirred.

HERSHEY'S HINT

To get the number of cookies listed in a drop cookie recipe, drop cookie dough with a tableware spoon, not a measuring spoon.

¾ cup sliced almonds, toasted*

1 cup (2 sticks) butter or margarine, softened

¾ cup sugar

3 egg yolks

¾ teaspoon almond extract

2 cups all-purpose flour

Raspberry Filling (recipe follows)

Powdered sugar (optional)

*To toast almonds: Heat oven to 350°F. Spread almonds in thin layer in shallow baking pan. Bake 8 to 10 minutes, stirring occasionally, until light golden brown; cool.

ALMOND SHORTBREAD COOKIES WITH RASPBERRY FILLING

Makes about 3¹/₂ dozen sandwich cookies

1. Finely chop almonds.

2. Beat butter and sugar until in large bowl creamy. Add egg yolks and almond extract; beat well. Gradually add flour, beating until well blended. Stir in almonds. Refrigerate dough 1 to 2 hours or until firm enough to handle.

3. Heat oven to 350°F.

4. On well-floured surface, roll about one-fourth of dough to about ¹/₈-inch thickness (keep remaining dough in refrigerator). Using 2-inch round cookie cutter, cut into equal number of rounds. Place on ungreased cookie sheet.

5. Bake 8 to 10 minutes or until almost set. Cool slightly; remove from cookie sheet to wire rack. Cool completely.

6. Meanwhile, prepare Raspberry Filling. Spread about one measuring teaspoon filling onto bottom of one cookie. Top with second cookie; gently press together. Repeat with remaining cookies. Allow to set about 1 hour. Lightly sift powdered sugar over top of cookies, if desired. Cover; store at room temperature.

RASPBERRY FILLING: In small saucepan over low heat, combine 1 cup HERSHEY'S Raspberry Chips and ¹/₃ cup whipping cream. Stir constantly until mixture is smooth. Remove from heat. Cool about 20 minutes or until slightly thickened and spreadable. Makes about 1 cup filling.

67

6 tablespoons butter or
  margarine, softened

½ cup packed light brown
  sugar

¼ cup granulated sugar

1 egg

1 teaspoon vanilla extract

1½ cups all-purpose flour

½ teaspoon baking soda

¼ teaspoon salt

2 cups (12-ounce package)
  HERSHEY'S Semi-Sweet
  Chocolate Chips

THREE-IN-ONE CHOCOLATE CHIP COOKIES

Beat butter, brown sugar and granulated sugar in large bowl until fluffy. Add egg and vanilla; beat well. Stir together flour, baking soda and salt; gradually blend into butter mixture. Stir in chocolate chips. Shape and bake cookies into one of the three versions below.

GIANT COOKIE: Prepare dough. Heat oven to 350°F. Line $12 \times 5/8$-inch round pizza pan with foil. Pat dough evenly into prepared pan to within $3/4$ inch of edge. Bake 15 to 18 minutes or until lightly browned. Cool completely; cut into wedges. Decorate or garnish as desired. Makes about 8 servings (one 12-inch cookie).

MEDIUM-SIZE REFRIGERATOR COOKIES: Prepare dough. On wax paper, shape into 2 rolls, $1^1/2$ inches in diameter. Wrap in wax paper; cover with plastic wrap. Refrigerate several hours or until firm enough to slice. Heat oven to 350°F. Remove rolls from refrigerator; remove wrapping. With sharp knife, cut into $1/4$-inch-wide slices. Place on ungreased cookie sheet, about 3 inches apart. Bake 8 to 10 minutes or until lightly browned. Cool slightly; remove from cookie sheet to wire racks. Cool completely. Makes about $2^1/2$ dozen ($2^1/2$-inch) cookies.

continued on page 70

Giant Three-in-One Chocolate Chip Cookie

70

2¼ cups all-purpose flour

1 teaspoon baking soda

½ teaspoon salt

¾ cup (1½ sticks) butter or margarine, softened

¾ cup granulated sugar

¾ cup packed light brown sugar

1 teaspoon vanilla extract

2 eggs

1 cup SKOR English Toffee Bits *or* 1 cup HEATH BITS 'O BRICKLE Almond Toffee Bits

1 cup HERSHEY'S Semi-Sweet Chocolate Chips

Three-in-One Chocolate Chip Cookies, continued

MINIATURE COOKIES: Prepare dough. Heat oven to 350°F. Drop dough by ¼ teaspoons onto ungreased cookie sheet, about 1½ inches apart. (Or, spoon dough into disposable plastic frosting bag; cut about ¼ inch off tip. Squeeze dough by ¼ teaspoons onto ungreased cookie sheet.) Bake 5 to 7 minutes or just until set. Cool slightly; remove from cookie sheet to wire racks. Cool completely. Makes about 18½ dozen (¾-inch) cookies.

SKOR BITS & CHOCOLATE CHIP COOKIES

Makes about 4 dozen cookies

1. Heat oven to 375°F.

2. Stir together flour, baking soda and salt in medium bowl. Beat butter, granulated sugar, brown sugar and vanilla in large bowl until well blended. Add eggs; beat well. Gradually add flour mixture, beating well. Stir in toffee bits and chocolate chips. Drop dough by rounded teaspoons onto ungreased cookie sheet.

3. Bake 8 to 10 minutes or until lightly browned. Cool slightly; remove from cookie sheet to wire racks. Cool completely.

Prep Time: 25 minutes
Bake Time: 8 minutes
Cool Time: 30 minutes

½ cup (1 stick) butter or
   margarine, softened

1 cup sugar

2 eggs

½ teaspoon vanilla extract

½ teaspoon walnut extract

2½ cups all-purpose flour

1 teaspoon baking powder

¼ teaspoon salt

1 cup HERSHEY'S MINI CHIPS
   Semi-Sweet Chocolate

1 cup ground walnuts

WALNUT MINI CHIP BISCOTTI

Makes about 4 dozen biscotti

1. Heat oven to 350°F.

2. Beat butter and sugar in large bowl until well blended. Add eggs, vanilla and walnut extract; beat until smooth. Stir together flour, baking powder and salt; gradually add to butter mixture, beating until smooth. (Dough will be thick.) Using wooden spoon, work Mini Chips and walnuts into dough. Divide dough into four equal parts. Shape each part into a log about 9 inches long. Place logs on ungreased cookie sheet, at least 2 inches apart.

3. Bake 25 minutes or until logs are set. Remove from oven; let cool on cookie sheet 15 minutes. Using serrated knife and sawing motion, cut logs diagonally into $1/2$-inch slices. Discard end pieces. Arrange slices cut sides down and close together on cookie sheet.

4. Bake 5 to 6 minutes. Turn each slice over; bake an additional 5 to 6 minutes. Remove from oven; cool on cookie sheet.

1 ¼ cups all-purpose flour

1 cup sugar

⅛ teaspoon salt

¾ cup (1 ½ sticks) butter, melted (no substitutes)

⅓ cup HERSHEY'S Cocoa

3 eggs

2 egg yolks

½ teaspoon vanilla extract

Chocolate Frosting (recipe follows)

CHOCOLATE MADELEINES

Makes about 1½ dozen filled cookies

1. Heat oven to 350°F. Lightly grease indentations of madeleine mold pan (each shell is 3×2 inches).

2. Stir together flour, sugar and salt in medium saucepan. Combine melted butter and cocoa; stir into dry ingredients. In small bowl, lightly beat eggs, egg yolks and vanilla with fork until well blended; stir into chocolate mixture, blending well. Cook over very low heat, stirring constantly, until mixture is warm. Do not simmer or boil. Remove from heat. Fill each mold ½ full with batter. (Do not overfill.)

3. Bake 8 to 10 minutes or until wooden pick inserted in centers comes out clean. Invert onto wire racks; cool completely. Prepare Chocolate Frosting; frost flat sides of cookies. Press frosted sides together, forming shells.

CHOCOLATE FROSTING

Makes about ¾ cup

1 ¼ cups powdered sugar

2 tablespoons HERSHEY'S Cocoa

2 tablespoons butter, softened (no substitutes)

2 to 2 ½ tablespoons milk

½ teaspoon vanilla extract

Stir together powdered sugar and cocoa in small bowl. In another small bowl, beat butter and ¼ cup of the cocoa mixture until fluffy. Gradually add remaining cocoa mixture alternately with milk, beating to spreading consistency. Stir in vanilla.

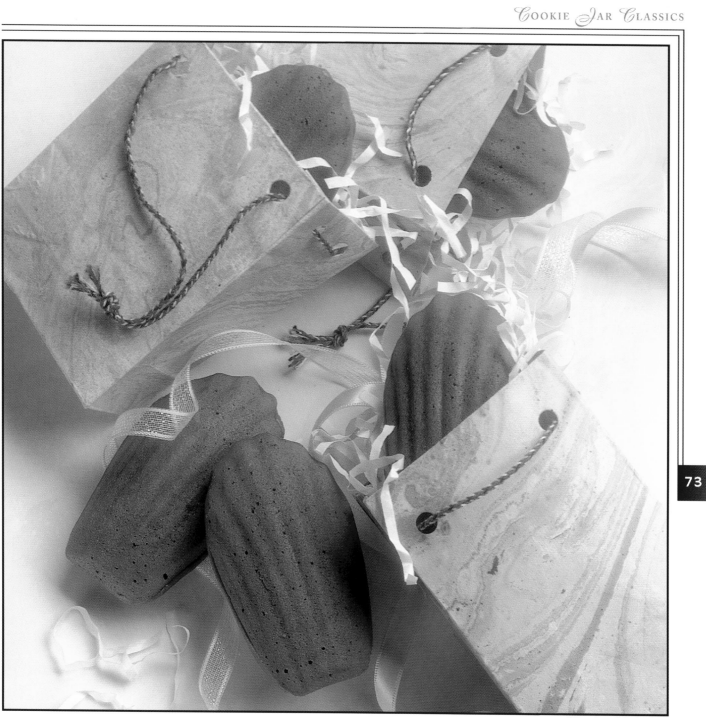

Chocolate Madeleines

½ cup (1 stick) butter or margarine, softened

⅔ cup sugar

1 egg, separated

2 tablespoons milk

1 teaspoon vanilla extract

1 cup all-purpose flour

⅓ cup HERSHEY'S Cocoa

¼ teaspoon salt

1 cup chopped nuts

Vanilla Filling (recipe follows)

26 HERSHEY'S KISSES Milk Chocolates, HERSHEY'S HUGS Chocolates, pecan halves or candied cherry halves

CHOCOLATE THUMBPRINT COOKIES

Makes about 2 dozen cookies

1. Beat butter, sugar, egg yolk, milk and vanilla in medium bowl until fluffy. Stir together flour, cocoa and salt; gradually add to butter mixture, beating until blended. Refrigerate dough at least 1 hour or until firm enough to handle.

2. Heat oven to 350°F. Lightly grease cookie sheet. Shape dough into 1-inch balls. With fork, beat egg white slightly. Dip each ball into egg white; roll in nuts. Place on prepared cookie sheet. Press thumb gently in center of each cookie.

3. Bake cookies 10 to 12 minutes or until set. Meanwhile, prepare Vanilla Filling. Remove wrappers from chocolate pieces. Remove cookies from cookie sheet to wire rack; cool 5 minutes. Spoon about $1/4$ teaspoon prepared filling into each thumbprint. Gently press chocolate piece onto top of each cookie. Cool completely.

VANILLA FILLING

Makes about $1/3$ cup

½ cup powdered sugar

1 tablespoon butter or margarine, softened

2 teaspoons milk

¼ teaspoon vanilla extract

Combine powdered sugar, butter, milk and vanilla; beat until smooth.

1 HERSHEY'S Cookies 'n' Mint
   Milk Chocolate Bar
   (7 ounces)

½ cup (1 stick) butter or
   margarine, softened

¾ cup sugar

1 egg

1 teaspoon vanilla extract

1 cup all-purpose flour

⅓ cup HERSHEY'S Cocoa

½ teaspoon baking soda

⅛ teaspoon salt

1 cup coarsely chopped nuts
   (optional)

DOUBLY CHOCOLATE MINT COOKIES

Makes about 2¹/₂ dozen cookies

1. Heat oven to 350°F.

2. Cut chocolate bar into small pieces; set aside. Beat butter, sugar, egg and vanilla in large bowl until fluffy. Combine flour, cocoa, baking soda and salt in separate bowl; add butter mixture, beating until well blended. Stir in chocolate and nuts, if desired. Drop rounded teaspoons onto ungreased cookie sheet.

3. Bake 10 to 12 minutes or until set. Cool slightly; remove to wire racks. Cool completely.

75

½ cup (1 stick) butter or margarine, softened

1 package (3 ounces) cream cheese, softened

1 cup all-purpose flour

1 egg

⅔ cup packed light brown sugar

1 tablespoon butter, melted

1 teaspoon vanilla extract

Dash salt

72 HERSHEY'S MINI KISSES Milk Chocolate Baking Pieces, divided

½ to ¾ cup coarsely chopped pecans

PECAN MINI KISSES CUPS

Makes 2 dozen cups

1. Beat ½ cup softened butter and cream cheese in medium bowl until blended. Add flour; beat well. Cover; refrigerate about 1 hour or until firm enough to handle.

2. Heat oven to 325°F. Stir together egg, brown sugar, 1 tablespoon melted butter, vanilla and salt in small bowl until well blended.

3. Shape chilled dough into 24 balls (1 inch each). Place balls in ungreased small muffin cups (1¾ inches in diameter). Press onto bottoms and up sides of cups. Place 2 Mini Kisses in each cup. Spoon about 1 teaspoon pecans over chocolate. Fill each cup with egg mixture.

4. Bake 25 minutes or until filling is set. Lightly press 1 Mini Kiss into center of each cookie. Cool in pan on wire rack.

HERSHEY'S HINT

Shiny pans are preferred for baking cookies and bars since they reflect heat and will produce light, delicate treats.

Pecan Mini Kisses Cups

2¼ cups all-purpose flour

⅓ cup HERSHEY'S Cocoa

1 teaspoon baking soda

½ teaspoon salt

1 cup (2 sticks) butter or margarine, softened

¾ cup granulated sugar

¾ cup packed light brown sugar

1 teaspoon vanilla extract

2 eggs

2 cups (12-ounce package) HERSHEY'S Semi-Sweet Chocolate Chips

1 cup chopped nuts (optional)

HERSHEY'S "PERFECTLY CHOCOLATE" CHOCOLATE CHIP COOKIES

Makes about 5 dozen cookies

1. Heat oven to 375°F.

2. Stir together flour, cocoa, baking soda and salt. Beat butter, granulated sugar, brown sugar and vanilla in large bowl on medium speed of mixer until creamy. Add eggs; beat well. Gradually add flour mixture, beating until well blended. Stir in chocolate chips and nuts, if desired. Drop by rounded teaspoons onto ungreased cookie sheet.

3. Bake 8 to 10 minutes or until set. Cool slightly; remove from cookie sheet to wire racks.

HERSHEY'S HINT

Bake cookies on the middle rack of the oven, one pan at a time. Uneven browning can occur if baking on more than one rack at the same time.

Hershey's *"Perfectly Chocolate"* Chocolate Chip Cookies

2¼ cups all-purpose flour

1 teaspoon baking soda

½ teaspoon salt

1 cup (2 sticks) butter, softened

¾ cup granulated sugar

¾ cup packed light brown sugar

1 teaspoon vanilla extract

2 eggs

2 cups (12-ounce package) HERSHEY'S Semi-Sweet Chocolate Chips

1 cup chopped nuts (optional)

HERSHEY'S CLASSIC CHOCOLATE CHIP COOKIES

Makes 5 dozen cookies

1. Heat oven to 375° F.

2. Stir together flour, baking soda and salt. Beat butter, granulated sugar, brown sugar and vanilla in large bowl with mixer until creamy. Add eggs; beat well. Gradually add flour mixture, beating well. Stir in chocolate chips and nuts, if desired. Drop by rounded teaspoons onto greased cookie sheet.

3. Bake 8 to 10 minutes or until lightly browned. Cool slightly; remove from cookie sheet to wire racks. Cool completely.

PAN RECIPE: Spread batter into greased $15^{1}/_{2} \times 10^{1}/_{2} \times 1$-inch jelly-roll pan. Bake at 375°F 20 minutes or until lightly browned. Cool completely. Cut into bars. Makes about 48 bars.

ICE CREAM SANDWICHES: Press one small scoop of vanilla ice cream between two cookies.

HIGH ALTITUDE DIRECTIONS: Increase flour to $2^{2}/_{3}$ cups. Decrease baking soda to $^{3}/_{4}$ teaspoon. Decrease granulated sugar to $^{2}/_{3}$ cup. Decrease packed light brown sugar to $^{2}/_{3}$ cup. Add $^{1}/_{2}$ teaspoon water with flour. Bake at 375°F 5 to 7 minutes or until tops are light golden with golden brown edges.

1 cup (2 sticks) butter or margarine, softened

⅔ cup powdered sugar

⅓ cup HERSHEY'S Cocoa

1 teaspoon vanilla extract

⅛ teaspoon salt

1⅔ cups all-purpose flour

1 cup walnuts, finely chopped

1⅔ cups (10-ounce package) HERSHEY'S Premier White Chips

1 tablespoon shortening (do not use butter, margarine, spread or oil)

1 cup HERSHEY'S Semi-Sweet Chocolate Chips, melted

COCOA-WALNUT CRESCENTS

Makes about 6 dozen cookies

1. Beat butter and sugar in large bowl until fluffy. Add cocoa, vanilla and salt; mix on low speed of mixer until blended. Mix in flour and walnuts. Cover; refrigerate dough 1 hour.

2. Heat oven to 325°F. Grease cookie sheet. Divide dough into 6 portions. Working with one portion at a time, shape into 18-inch-long rope; cut into 12 (1½-inch) pieces. Form into crescent shapes, tapering ends. Place on cookie sheet. Repeat with remaining dough.

3. Bake 15 to 18 minutes. Remove from cookie sheet to wire racks; cool completely.

4. Place white chips and shortening in microwave-safe bowl. Microwave at HIGH (100%) 1 minute or until chips are softened; stir. Microwave at HIGH an additional 15 seconds at a time, stirring after each heating, just until chips are melted when stirred.

5. Dip crescents halfway into melted white chips; place on wax paper until set. Drizzle coated ends of crescents with melted semi-sweet chips. Allow to stand until set.

81

1⅔ cups (10-ounce package) HERSHEY'S Premier White Chips, divided

2¼ cups all-purpose flour

¾ cup sugar

2 eggs

¾ teaspoon baking soda

½ teaspoon freshly grated lemon peel

¼ teaspoon lemon extract

½ cup (1 stick) butter or margarine

¾ cup chopped pecans

Lemon Drizzle (recipe follows)

LEMON PECAN COOKIES

Makes about 3½ dozen cookies

1. Heat oven to 350°F. Reserve 2 tablespoons white chips for drizzle.

2. Combine flour, sugar, eggs, baking soda, lemon peel and lemon extract in large bowl. Place remaining white chips and butter in medium microwave-safe bowl. Microwave at HIGH (100%) 1 minute; stir. If necessary, microwave at HIGH an additional 15 seconds at a time, stirring after each heating, just until chips and butter are melted when stirred. Add chip mixture to flour mixture; beat until blended. Stir in pecans. Drop dough by rounded teaspoons onto ungreased cookie sheet.

3. Bake 9 to 11 minutes or until very slightly golden around edges. Remove from cookie sheet to wire racks. Cool completely. Prepare Lemon Drizzle; lightly drizzle over cookies.

LEMON DRIZZLE

2 tablespoons HERSHEY'S Premier White Chips (reserved from cookies)

½ teaspoon shortening (do not use butter, margarine, spread or oil)

Yellow food color

Lemon extract (optional)

Place white chips and shortening in small microwave-safe bowl. Microwave at HIGH (100%) 30 seconds; stir. If necessary, microwave at HIGH an additional 15 seconds at a time, stirring after each heating, just until chips are melted when stirred. Stir in a few drops food color and a few drops lemon extract, if desired.

HERSHEY'S DOUBLY CHOCOLATE COOKIES

Makes about 4¹/₂ dozen cookies

1. Heat oven to 350°F.

2. Stir together flour, cocoa, baking soda and salt. Beat butter, sugar, eggs and vanilla in large bowl until fluffy. Gradually add flour mixture, beating well. Stir in chocolate chips and nuts, if desired. Drop by rounded teaspoons onto ungreased cookie sheet.

3. Bake 8 to 10 minutes or just until set. Cool slightly; remove from cookie sheet to wire racks. Cool completely.

2 cups all-purpose flour

²/₃ cup HERSHEY'S Cocoa

¾ teaspoon baking soda

¼ teaspoon salt

1 cup (2 sticks) butter or margarine, softened

1½ cups sugar

2 eggs

2 teaspoons vanilla extract

2 cups (12-ounce package) HERSHEY'S Semi-Sweet Chocolate Chips *or* 2 cups (11½-ounce package) HERSHEY'S Milk Chocolate Chips

½ cup coarsely chopped nuts (optional)

- ½ cup (1 stick) butter or margarine
- 1 cup REESE'S Peanut Butter Chips
- ⅔ cup packed light brown sugar
- 1 egg
- ¾ teaspoon vanilla extract
- 1⅓ cups all-purpose flour
- ¾ teaspoon baking soda
- ½ cup finely chopped pecans
- Chocolate Chip Glaze (recipe follows)

PEANUT BUTTER CUT-OUT COOKIES

Makes about 3 dozen cookies

1. Place butter and peanut butter chips in medium saucepan; cook over low heat, stirring constantly, until melted. Pour into large bowl; add brown sugar, egg and vanilla, beating until well blended. Stir in flour, baking soda and pecans, blending well. Refrigerate 15 to 20 minutes or until firm enough to roll.

2. Heat oven to 350°F.

3. Roll a small portion of dough at a time on lightly floured board, or between 2 pieces of wax paper to $1/4$-inch thickness. (Keep remaining dough in refrigerator.) With cookie cutters, cut dough into desired shapes; place on ungreased cookie sheets.

4. Bake 7 to 8 minutes or until almost set (do not overbake). Cool 1 minute; remove from cookie sheets to wire racks. Cool completely. Prepare Chocolate Chip Glaze; drizzle onto each cookie. Allow to set.

CHOCOLATE CHIP GLAZE: In small microwave-safe bowl, place 1 cup HERSHEY'S Semi-Sweet chocolate Chips and 1 tablespoon shortening (do not use butter, margarine, spread or oil). Microwave at HIGH (100%) 1 minute; stir. If necessary, microwave at HIGH an additional 15 seconds at a time, stirring after each heating, just until chips are melted and mixture is smooth.

Peanut Butter Cut-Out Cookies

1⅔ cups (10-ounce package) HERSHEY'S Raspberry Chips, divided

1 cup (2 sticks) butter or margarine, softened

1 cup packed light brown sugar

¾ cup granulated sugar

2 eggs

1 teaspoon vanilla extract

2½ cups all-purpose flour

⅓ cup HERSHEY'S Cocoa

1 teaspoon baking powder

1 teaspoon baking soda

1½ teaspoons shortening (do not use butter, margarine, spread or oil)

DRIZZLED RASPBERRY CRINKLES

Makes about 5 dozen cookies

1. Heat oven to 350°F.

2. Set aside ¹/₂ cup raspberry chips. In small microwave-safe bowl, place remaining chips. Microwave at HIGH (100%) 1 minute or until chips are melted when stirred.

3. Beat butter, brown sugar and granulated sugar in large bowl until well blended. Add melted chips; beat until well blended. Beat in eggs and vanilla. Stir together flour, cocoa, baking powder and baking soda. Gradually beat into chocolate mixture. Drop by rounded teaspoons onto ungreased cookie sheet.

4. Bake 8 to 9 minutes for chewy cookies or 10 to 11 minutes for crisp cookies. Cool slightly. Remove from cookie sheet to wire racks. Cool completely.

5. Place reserved chips and shortening in small microwave-safe bowl. Microwave at HIGH 30 seconds or until chips are melted when stirred. Drizzle over cookies.

87

Drizzled Raspberry Crinkles

1¾ cups all-purpose flour

1½ cups sugar

¾ cup (1½ sticks) butter or margarine, softened

⅔ cup HERSHEY'S Cocoa or HERSHEY'S Dutch Processed Cocoa

¾ teaspoon baking soda

¼ teaspoon salt

2 eggs

2 tablespoons milk

1 teaspoon vanilla extract

½ cup finely chopped pecans

Coconut and Pecan Filling (page 90)

FUDGEY GERMAN CHOCOLATE SANDWICH COOKIES

Makes about 1½ dozen sandwich cookies

1. Heat oven to 350°F.

2. Combine flour, sugar, butter, cocoa, baking soda, salt, eggs, milk and vanilla in large bowl. Beat at medium speed of mixer until blended (dough will be thick). Stir in pecans.

3. Form dough into 1¼-inch balls. Place on ungreased cookie sheet; flatten slightly.

4. Bake 9 to 11 minutes or until almost set. Cool slightly; remove from cookie sheet to wire racks. Cool completely. Prepare Coconut and Pecan Filling; spread about 1 heaping tablespoon onto bottom of one cookie. Top with second cookie to make sandwich. Serve warm or at room temperature. *continued on page 90*

Fudgey German Chocolate Sandwich Cookies

Fudgey German Chocolate Sandwich Cookies, continued

COCONUT AND PECAN FILLING

Makes about 2 cups filling

- ½ cup (1 stick) butter or margarine
- ½ cup packed light brown sugar
- ¼ cup light corn syrup
- 1 cup MOUNDS Sweetened Coconut Flakes, toasted*
- 1 cup finely chopped pecans
- 1 teaspoon vanilla extract

To toast coconut: Heat oven to 350°F. Spread coconut in even layer on baking sheet. Bake 6 to 8 minutes, stirring occasionally, until golden.

Melt butter in medium saucepan over medium heat; add brown sugar and corn syrup. Stir constantly, until thick and bubbly. Remove from heat; stir in coconut, pecans and vanilla. Use warm.

Prep Time: 25 minutes
Bake Time: 9 minutes
Cool Time: 35 minutes

½ cup (1 stick) butter or
    margarine, softened

¾ cup sugar

1 egg

1 teaspoon vanilla extract

1½ cups all-purpose flour

⅓ cup HERSHEY'S Cocoa

½ teaspoon baking powder

½ teaspoon baking soda

¼ teaspoon salt

    Vanilla Glaze (recipe follows)

CUT-OUT CHOCOLATE COOKIES

Makes about 3 dozen cookies

1. Beat butter, sugar, egg and vanilla in large bowl until fluffy. Combine flour, cocoa, baking powder, baking soda and salt; add to butter mixture, blending well. Chill dough about 1 hour or until firm enough to roll.

2. Heat oven to 325°F.

3. On lightly floured board or between 2 pieces of wax paper, roll small portion of dough at a time to $1/4$-inch thickness. Cut into desired shapes with cookie cutters; place on ungreased cookie sheet.

4. Bake 5 to 7 minutes or until no indentation remains when touched lightly. Cool slightly; remove from cookie sheet to wire racks. Cool completely. Frost with Vanilla Glaze. Decorate as desired.

VANILLA GLAZE

Makes about 1 cup glaze

    3 tablespoons butter or margarine

    2 cups powdered sugar

    1 teaspoon vanilla extract

    2 to 3 tablespoons milk

    2 to 4 drops food color (optional)

Melt butter in small saucepan over low heat. Remove from heat; blend in powdered sugar and vanilla. Add milk gradually, beating with spoon or wire whisk until glaze is of desired consistency. Blend in food color, if desired.

½ cup REESE'S Peanut Butter Chips

3 tablespoons plus ½ cup (1 stick) butter or margarine, softened and divided

1¼ cups sugar, divided

¼ cup light corn syrup

1 egg

1 teaspoon vanilla extract

2 cups plus 2 tablespoons all-purpose flour, divided

2 teaspoons baking soda

¼ teaspoon salt

½ cup HERSHEY'S Cocoa

5 tablespoons butter or margarine, melted

Additional sugar

About 2 dozen large marshmallows

PEANUT BUTTER AND CHOCOLATE COOKIE SANDWICH COOKIES

Makes about 2 dozen sandwich cookies

1. Heat oven to 350°F. Melt peanut butter chips and 3 tablespoons softened butter in small saucepan over very low heat. Remove from heat; cool slightly.

2. Beat remaining $1/2$ cup softened butter and 1 cup sugar in large bowl until fluffy. Add corn syrup, egg and vanilla; blend thoroughly. Stir together 2 cups flour, baking soda and salt; add to butter mixture, blending well. Remove $1^1/4$ cups dough and place in small bowl; with wooden spoon, stir in remaining 2 tablespoons flour and peanut butter chip mixture.

3. Blend cocoa, remaining $1/4$ cup sugar and 5 tablespoons melted butter into remaining dough. Refrigerate both doughs 5 to 10 minutes or until firm enough to handle. Roll each dough into 1-inch balls; roll in sugar. Place on ungreased cookie sheet.

4. Bake 10 to 11 minutes or until set. Cool slightly; remove from cookie sheet to wire racks. Cool completely. Place 1 marshmallow on flat side of 1 chocolate cookie. Microwave at MEDIUM (50%) 10 seconds or until marshmallow is softened; place a peanut butter cookie over marshmallow, pressing down slightly. Repeat for remaining cookies. Serve immediately.

Peanut Butter and Chocolate Cookie Sandwich Cookies

1 cup (2 sticks) butter or
  margarine, softened

2 cups sugar

2 eggs

2 teaspoons vanilla extract

2 cups all-purpose flour

¾ cup HERSHEY'S Cocoa

1 teaspoon baking soda

½ teaspoon salt

1⅔ cups (10-ounce package)
  HERSHEY'S Premier White
  Chips

HERSHEY'S WHITE CHIP CHOCOLATE COOKIES

Makes about 4¹/₂ dozen cookies

1. Heat oven to 350°F.

2. Beat butter and sugar in large bowl until creamy. Add eggs and vanilla; beat until fluffy. Stir together flour, cocoa, baking soda and salt; gradually blend into butter mixture. Stir in white chips. Drop by rounded teaspoons onto ungreased cookie sheet.

3. Bake 8 to 9 minutes. (Do not overbake; cookies will be soft. They will puff while baking and flatten upon cooling.) Cool slightly; remove from cookie sheet to wire racks. Cool completely.

HERSHEY'S HINT

Cool cookie sheets completely before putting more cookie dough on them. Dropping cookie dough on warm cookie sheets causes excess spread.

Hershey's White Chip Chocolate Cookies

½ cup (1 stick) butter or margarine, softened
¾ cup sugar
1 egg
1 teaspoon vanilla extract
1 ½ cups all-purpose flour
⅓ cup HERSHEY'S Cocoa
½ teaspoon baking powder
½ teaspoon baking soda
¼ teaspoon salt
Decorative Frosting (recipe follows)

GREETING CARD COOKIES

Makes about 1 dozen cookies

1. Beat butter, sugar, egg and vanilla in large bowl until fluffy. Stir together flour, cocoa, baking powder, baking soda and salt; add to butter mixture, blending well. Refrigerate about 1 hour or until firm enough to roll. Cut cardboard rectangle for pattern, $2^{1}/_{2} \times 4$ inches; wrap in plastic wrap.

2. Heat oven to 350°F. Lightly grease cookie sheet. On lightly floured board or between two pieces of wax paper, roll out half of dough to $^{1}/_{4}$-inch thickness. For each cookie, place pattern on dough; cut through dough around pattern with sharp paring knife. (Save dough trimmings and reroll for remaining cookies.) Carefully place cutouts on prepared cookie sheet.

3. Bake 8 to 10 minutes or until set. Cool 1 minute on cookie sheet. (If cookies have lost their shape, trim irregular edges while cookies are still hot.) Carefully transfer to wire racks. Repeat procedure with remaining dough.

4. Prepare Decorative Frosting; spoon into pastry bag fitted with decorating tip. Pipe names or greetings onto cookies; decorate as desired.

DECORATIVE FROSTING
Makes about 1³/₄ cup

> 3 cups powdered sugar
> ⅓ cup shortening
> 2 to 3 tablespoons milk
> Food color (optional)

Beat powdered sugar and shortening in small bowl; gradually add milk, beating until smooth and slightly thickened. Cover until ready to use. If desired, divide frosting into two bowls; tint with food color.

MACAROON KISS COOKIES
Makes about 4¹/₂ dozen cookies

⅓ cup butter or margarine, softened
1 package (3 ounces) cream cheese, softened
¾ cup sugar
1 egg yolk
2 teaspoons almond extract
2 teaspoons orange juice
1 ¼ cups all-purpose flour
2 teaspoons baking powder
¼ teaspoon salt
5 cups MOUNDS Sweetened Coconut Flakes, divided
1 bag (8 ounces) HERSHEY'S KISSES Milk Chocolates

1. Beat together butter, cream cheese and sugar in large bowl. Add egg yolk, almond extract and orange juice; beat well. Stir together flour, baking powder and salt; gradually add to butter mixture. Stir in 3 cups coconut. Cover; refrigerate 1 hour or until firm enough to handle.

2. Heat oven to 350°F. Shape dough into 1-inch balls; roll in remaining 2 cups coconut. Place on ungreased cookie sheets.

3. Bake 10 to 12 minutes or until lightly browned. Meanwhile, remove wrappers from chocolate pieces. Remove cookies from oven; immediately press chocolate piece in center of each cookie. Cool 1 minute. Carefully remove from cookie sheets to wire racks. Cool completely.

97

BROWNIES AND BARS

¾ cup (1½ sticks) butter or margarine, softened

¾ cup packed light brown sugar

½ cup granulated sugar

2 eggs

2 cups all-purpose flour

1 teaspoon baking soda

½ teaspoon salt

1⅔ cups (10-ounce package) HERSHEY'S Butterscotch Chips

1 cup chopped nuts (optional)

BUTTERSCOTCH BLONDIES

Makes about 36 bars

1. Heat oven to 350°F. Grease 13×9×2-inch baking pan.

2. Beat butter, brown sugar and granulated sugar in large bowl until creamy. Add eggs; beat well. Stir together flour, baking soda and salt; gradually add to butter mixture, blending well. Stir in butterscotch chips and nuts, if desired. Spread into prepared pan.

3. Bake 30 to 35 minutes or until top is golden brown and center is set. Cool completely in pan on wire rack. Cut into bars.

Butterscotch Blondies

1½ cups all-purpose flour

½ cup packed light brown sugar

½ cup (1 stick) cold butter or margarine

1⅔ cups (10-ounce package) REESE'S Peanut Butter Chips, divided

1 can (14 ounces) sweetened condensed milk (not evaporated milk)

1 egg, slightly beaten

1 teaspoon vanilla extract

¾ cup chopped walnuts

Powdered sugar (optional)

PEANUT BUTTER CHIP TRIANGLES

Makes 24 or 40 triangles

1. Heat oven to 350°F. Stir together flour and brown sugar in medium bowl. Cut in butter with pastry blender or fork until mixture resembles coarse crumbs. Stir in $1/2$ cup peanut butter chips. Press mixture onto bottom of ungreased 13×9×2-inch baking pan. Bake 15 minutes.

2. Meanwhile, combine sweetened condensed milk, egg and vanilla in large bowl. Stir in remaining chips and walnuts. Spread evenly over hot baked crust.

3. Bake 25 minutes or until golden brown. Cool completely in pan on wire rack. Cut into 2- or $2^1/_2$-inch squares; cut squares diagonally into triangles. Sift powdered sugar over top, if desired.

Prep Time: 20 minutes
Bake Time: 40 minutes
Cool Time: 2 hours

TIP: To sprinkle powdered sugar over brownies, bars, cupcakes or other desserts, place sugar in a wire mesh strainer. Hold over top of desserts and gently tap sides of strainer.

Peanut Butter Chip Triangles

6 tablespoons butter (do not
use margarine)

½ cup HERSHEY'S Cocoa

2 cups powdered sugar

3 tablespoons plus
1 teaspoon milk, divided

1 teaspoon vanilla extract

Mint Filling (recipe follows)

CHOCOLATE MINT SQUARES

Makes about 48 pieces

1. Line 8-inch square pan with foil, extending foil over edges of pan.

2. Melt butter in small saucepan over low heat; add cocoa. Cook, stirring constantly, just until mixture is smooth. Remove from heat; add powdered sugar, 3 tablespoons milk and vanilla. Cook over low heat, stirring constantly, until mixture is glossy. Spread half of mixture into prepared pan. Refrigerate.

3. Meanwhile, prepare Mint Filling; spread filling over chocolate layer. Refrigerate 10 minutes.

4. To remaining chocolate mixture in saucepan, add remaining 1 teaspoon milk. Cook over low heat, stirring constantly, until smooth. Spread quickly over filling. Refrigerate until firm. Use foil to lift candy out of pan; peel off foil. Cut candy into squares. Store in tightly covered container in refrigerator.

MINT FILLING

- **1 package (3 ounces) cream cheese, softened**
- **2 cups powdered sugar**
- **½ teaspoon vanilla extract**
- **¼ teaspoon peppermint extract**
- **3 to 5 drops green food color**
- **Milk**

Beat cream cheese, powdered sugar, vanilla, peppermint extract and food color in small bowl until smooth. Add 2 to 3 teaspoons milk, if needed, for spreading consistency.

HERSHEY'S HINT

Rich, buttery bar cookies and brownies freeze extremely well. Freeze in airtight containers or freezer bags for up to three months. Thaw at room temperature.

2 cups packed light brown sugar

1 cup (2 sticks) butter or margarine, melted

2 eggs

2 teaspoons vanilla extract

2 cups all-purpose flour

1 teaspoon salt

⅔ cup (of each) HERSHEY'S Semi-Sweet Chocolate Chips, REESE'S Peanut Butter Chips, and HERSHEY'S Premier White Chips

Chocolate Chip Drizzle (recipe follows)

THREE GREAT TASTES BLOND BROWNIES

Makes about 72 bars

1. Heat oven to 350°F. Grease 15½×10½×1-inch jelly-roll pan.

2. Stir together brown sugar and butter in large bowl; beat in eggs and vanilla until smooth. Add flour and salt, beating just until blended; stir in chocolate, peanut butter and white chips. Spread batter into prepared pan.

3. Bake 25 to 30 minutes or until wooden pick inserted in center comes out clean. Cool completely in pan on wire rack. Cut into bars. Prepare Chocolate Chip Drizzle; with tines of fork, drizzle randomly over bars.

CHOCOLATE CHIP DRIZZLE: In small microwave-safe bowl, place ¼ cup HERSHEY'S Semi-Sweet Chocolate Chips and ¼ teaspoon shortening (do not use butter, margarine, spread or oil). Microwave at HIGH (100%) 30 seconds to 1 minute; stir until chips are melted and mixture is smooth.

Three Great Tastes Blond Brownies

1 ¼ cups all-purpose flour, divided

1 cup granulated sugar, divided

⅓ cup butter, softened

¾ cup HERSHEY'S Premier White Chips

2 eggs, slightly beaten

¼ cup lemon juice

2 teaspoons freshly grated lemon peel

Powdered sugar

WHITE CHIP LEMON BARS

Makes about 36 bars

1. Heat oven to 350°F.

2. Stir together 1 cup flour and ¼ cup granulated sugar in medium bowl. Cut in butter with pastry blender or two knives until mixture resembles coarse crumbs. Press mixture onto bottom of 9-inch square baking pan.

3. Bake 15 minutes or until lightly browned. Remove from oven; sprinkle white chips over crust.

4. Stir together eggs, lemon juice, lemon peel, remaining ¼ cup flour and remaining ¾ cup granulated sugar in medium bowl; carefully pour over chips and crust.

5. Bake 15 minutes or until set. Cool slightly in pan on wire rack; sift with powdered sugar. Cool completely. Cut into bars.

White Chip Lemon Bars

½ cup (1 stick) butter or
    margarine, softened

½ cup shortening

1 cup packed light brown
    sugar

½ cup granulated sugar

2 eggs

1 teaspoon vanilla extract

½ teaspoon baking soda

2½ cups all-purpose flour

1¾ cups (10-ounce package)
    HERSHEY'S MINI KISSES
    Milk Chocolate Baking
    Pieces, divided

1 cup chopped nuts (optional)

MINI KISSES COOKIE BARS

Makes about 48 bars

1. Heat oven to 375°F. Beat butter and shortening in large bowl on medium speed of mixer just until blended.

2. Add brown sugar and granulated sugar; beat well. Beat in eggs, vanilla and baking soda. Gradually beat in flour (if dough becomes too stiff, stir in remaining flour with spoon). Set aside $^1/_2$ cup Mini Kisses; stir in remaining Mini Kisses and nuts, if desired. Press dough into ungreased $15^1/_2 \times 10^1/_2 \times 1$-inch jelly-roll pan.

3. Bake 15 to 20 minutes or until top is golden. Remove from oven; immediately place reserved Mini Kisses on top, pressing down lightly. Cool completely in pan on wire rack. Cut into bars.

Prep Time: 20 minutes
Bake Time: 15 minutes
Cool Time: 2 hours

⅓ cup butter or margarine

1½ bars (1 ounce each)
HERSHEY'S Unsweetened
Baking Chocolate

1 cup sugar

2 eggs

1 teaspoon vanilla extract

1 cup all-purpose flour

½ teaspoon baking powder

¼ teaspoon salt

1⅓ cups (8-ounce package)
HEATH BITS

ALL AMERICAN HEATH BROWNIES

Makes about 12 brownies

1. Heat oven to 350°F. Grease bottom of 8-inch square baking pan.

2. Melt butter and chocolate in medium saucepan over low heat, stirring occasionally. Stir in sugar. Add eggs, one at a time, beating after each addition. Stir in vanilla. Combine flour, baking powder and salt; add to chocolate mixture, stirring until well blended. Spread batter into prepared pan.

3. Bake 20 minutes or until brownie starts to pull away from edge of pan. Remove from oven; sprinkle with Heath Bits. Cover tightly with foil and cool completely on wire rack. Remove foil; cut into squares.

HERSHEY'S HINT

Brownies and bar cookies make great gifts. Place them in a paper-lined tin or on a decorative plate covered with plastic wrap and tied with a colorful ribbon. For a special touch, include the recipe.

4 eggs

1 ¼ cups sugar

½ cup (1 stick) butter or margarine, melted

2 teaspoons vanilla extract

1 ⅓ cups all-purpose flour

⅔ cup HERSHEY'S Cocoa

1 teaspoon baking powder

½ teaspoon salt

1 ⅔ cups (10-ounce package) HERSHEY'S Premier White Chips

HERSHEY'S WHITE CHIP BROWNIES

Makes about 36 brownies

1. Heat oven to 350°F. Grease 13×9×2-inch baking pan.

2. Beat eggs in large bowl until foamy; gradually beat in sugar. Add butter and vanilla; beat until blended. Stir together flour, cocoa, baking powder and salt; add to egg mixture, beating until blended. Stir in white chips. Spread batter into prepared pan.

3. Bake 25 to 30 minutes or until brownies begin to pull away from sides of pan. Cool completely in pan on wire rack. Cut into squares.

Prep Time: 15 minutes
Bake Time: 25 minutes
Cool Time: 2 hours

TIP: Brownies and bar cookies cut into different shapes can add interest to a plate of simple square cookies. Cut cookies into different-size rectangles or make triangles by cutting them into 2- to 2¹/₂-inch squares; cut each square in half diagonally. To make diamond shapes, cut straight lines 1 or 1¹/₂ inches apart the length of the baking pan; then cut straight lines 1¹/₂ inches apart diagonally across the pan.

Hershey's White Chip Brownies

½ cup sugar

2 tablespoons butter or margarine

2 tablespoons water

2 cups (12-ounce package) HERSHEY'S Semi-Sweet Chocolate Chips, divided

2 eggs

1 teaspoon vanilla extract

⅔ cup all-purpose flour

¼ teaspoon baking soda

¼ teaspoon salt

Caramel Topping (recipe follows)

1 cup pecan pieces

BROWNIE CARAMEL PECAN BARS

Makes about 16 bars

1. Heat oven to 350°F. Line 9-inch square baking pan with foil, extending foil over edges of pan. Grease and flour foil.

2. In medium saucepan, combine sugar, butter and water; cook over low heat, stirring constantly, until mixture boils. Remove from heat. Immediately add 1 cup chocolate chips; stir until melted. Beat in eggs and vanilla until well blended. Stir together flour, baking soda and salt; stir into chocolate mixture. Spread batter into prepared pan.

3. Bake 15 to 20 minutes or until brownies begin to pull away from sides of pan. Meanwhile, prepare Caramel Topping. Remove brownies from oven; immediately and carefully spread with prepared topping. Sprinkle remaining 1 cup chips and pecans over topping. Cool completely in pan on wire rack, being careful not to disturb chips while soft. Lift out of pan. Cut into bars.

CARAMEL TOPPING: Remove wrappers from 25 caramels. In medium microwave-safe bowl, place ¼ cup (½ stick) butter or margarine, caramels and 2 tablespoons milk. Microwave at HIGH (100%) 1 minute; stir. Microwave an additional 1 to 2 minutes, stirring every 30 seconds, or until caramels are melted and mixture is smooth when stirred. Use immediately.

Brownie Caramel Pecan Bars

½ cup sugar

¼ cup evaporated milk

¼ cup (½ stick) butter or margarine

8 bars (8-ounce package) HERSHEY'S Semi-Sweet Baking Chocolate, broken into pieces

2 eggs

1 teaspoon vanilla extract

¾ cup all-purpose flour

¼ teaspoon baking soda

¼ teaspoon salt

Brownie Frosting (recipe follows, optional)

RICH QUICK & EASY CHOCOLATE BROWNIES

Makes about 16 brownies

1. Heat oven to 325°F. Grease 9-inch square baking pan.

2. Combine sugar, evaporated milk and butter in medium saucepan. Cook over medium heat, stirring constantly, until mixture boils; remove from heat. Add chocolate, stirring until melted. Beat in eggs and vanilla. Stir in flour, baking soda and salt until well blended; pour into prepared pan.

3. Bake 30 to 35 minutes or until brownies just begin to pull away from sides of pan. Cool completely in pan on wire rack. Prepare Brownie Frosting; frost brownies, if desired. Cut into squares.

BROWNIE FROSTING

Makes about 1 cup frosting

2 bars (1 ounce each) HERSHEY'S Unsweetened
    Baking Chocolate, broken into pieces

2 tablespoons butter or margarine

1¾ cups powdered sugar

⅛ teaspoon salt

½ teaspoon vanilla extract

2 to 3 tablespoons water

Place chocolate and butter in small microwave-safe bowl.
Microwave at HIGH (100%) 1 minute; stir. If necessary,
microwave an additional 10 seconds at a time, stirring after
each heating, just until chocolate is melted when stirred.
Combine powdered sugar and salt in medium bowl. Stir in
chocolate mixture and vanilla. Add water; beat with spoon
to spreading consistency.

Prep Time: 30 minutes
Bake Time: 30 minutes
Cool Time: 2 hours

115

1 cup (2 sticks) butter or
  margarine, softened
½ cup packed light brown
  sugar
½ cup granulated sugar
2 eggs
1 teaspoon vanilla extract
1½ cups all-purpose flour
1 teaspoon baking soda
½ teaspoon salt
½ teaspoon ground cinnamon
3 cups quick-cooking or
  regular rolled oats
1¾ cups (10-ounce package)
  SKOR English Toffee Bits
  or 1¾ cups HEATH BITS
  'O BRICKLE, divided

OATMEAL TOFFEE BARS

Makes about 36 bars

1. Heat oven to 350°F. Grease 13×9×2-inch baking pan.

2. Beat butter, brown sugar and granulated sugar in large bowl until well blended. Add eggs and vanilla; beat well. Stir together flour, baking soda, salt and cinnamon; gradually add to butter mixture, beating until well blended. Stir in oats and $1^{1}/_{3}$ cups toffee bits (mixture will be stiff). Spread mixture into prepared pan.

3. Bake 25 minutes or until wooden pick inserted in center comes out clean. Immediately sprinkle remaining toffee bits over surface. Cool completely in pan on wire rack. Cut into bars.

Oatmeal Toffee Bars

½ cup (1 stick) butter or
    margarine, melted

1 cup sugar

1 teaspoon vanilla extract

2 eggs

½ cup all-purpose flour

⅓ cup HERSHEY'S Cocoa

¼ teaspoon baking powder

¼ teaspoon salt

½ cup chopped nuts (optional)

Creamy Brownie Frosting
    (recipe follows)

BEST BROWNIES

Makes about 16 brownies

1. Heat oven to 350°F. Grease 9-inch square baking pan.

2. Stir together butter, sugar and vanilla in large bowl. Add eggs; beat well with spoon. Combine flour, cocoa, baking powder and salt; gradually add to butter mixture, beating until well blended. Stir in nuts, if desired. Spread into prepared pan.

3. Bake 20 to 25 minutes or until brownies begin to pull away from sides of pan. Cool. Prepare Creamy Brownie Frosting; frost. Cut into squares.

CREAMY BROWNIE FROSTING

Makes about 1 cup frosting

3 tablespoons butter or margarine, softened

3 tablespoons HERSHEY'S Cocoa

1 tablespoon light corn syrup or honey

½ teaspoon vanilla extract

1 cup powdered sugar

1 to 2 tablespoons milk

Beat butter, cocoa, corn syrup and vanilla in small bowl. Add powdered sugar and milk; beat to spreading consistency.

From left to right: Best Brownies, Peanut Butter Chips and Jelly Bars (page 120)

1½ cups all-purpose flour

½ cup sugar

¾ teaspoon baking powder

½ cup (1 stick) cold butter or margarine

1 egg, beaten

¾ cup grape jelly

1⅔ cups (10-ounce package) REESE'S Peanut Butter Chips, divided

PEANUT BUTTER CHIPS AND JELLY BARS

Makes about 16 bars

1. Heat oven to 375°F. Grease 9-inch square baking pan.

2. Stir together flour, sugar and baking powder in large bowl. With pastry blender or two knives, cut in butter until mixture resembles coarse crumbs. Add egg; blend well. Reserve half of mixture; press remaining mixture onto bottom of prepared pan. Spread jelly over crust. Sprinkle 1 cup peanut butter chips over jelly. Stir together reserved crumb mixture with remaining ⅔ cup chips; sprinkle over top.

3. Bake 25 to 30 minutes or until lightly browned. Cool completely in pan on wire rack. Cut into bars.

TIP: For a whimsical twist on this tried-and-true classic, use cookie cutters to cut out shapes.

1½ cups finely crushed thin pretzels or pretzel sticks

¾ cup (1½ sticks) butter or margarine, melted

1 can (14 ounces) sweetened condensed milk (not evaporated milk)

1¾ cups (10-ounce package) HERSHEY'S MINI KISSES Semi-Sweet Chocolate Baking Pieces

3 cups miniature marshmallows

1⅓ cups coarsely chopped pecans or pecan pieces

ROCKY ROAD TASTY TEAM TREATS

Makes about 36 bars

1. Heat oven to 350°F. Grease bottom and sides of 13×9×2-inch baking pan.

2. Combine pretzels and melted butter in small bowl; press evenly onto bottom of prepared pan. Spread sweetened condensed milk evenly over pretzel layer; layer evenly with Mini Kisses, marshmallows and pecans, in order. Press down firmly on pecans.

3. Bake 20 to 25 minutes or until lightly browned. Cool completely in pan on wire rack. Cut into bars.

HERSHEY'S HINT

Why not try these tasty treats the next time you're called upon to prepare dessert for a tailgate party at the big game? Celebrate the team's victory with these easy-to-prepare and fun-to-eat bars.

121

1 ½ cups all-purpose flour

½ cup sugar

½ teaspoon baking powder

½ teaspoon salt

½ cup (1 stick) butter or margarine, softened

1 egg, beaten

¼ cup milk

¼ teaspoon vanilla extract

¾ cup raspberry preserves

1 cup HERSHEY'S Semi-Sweet Chocolate Chips

CHOCOLATE CHIPS AND RASPBERRY BARS

Makes about 32 bars

1. Heat oven to 400°F. Grease 13×9×2-inch baking pan.

2. Stir together flour, sugar, baking powder and salt in large bowl. Cut in butter with pastry blender or two knives until mixture resembles coarse crumbs. Add egg, milk and vanilla; beat on medium speed of mixer until well blended.

3. Reserve $^1/_2$ cup mixture for topping. Spread remaining mixture onto bottom of prepared pan (this will be a very thin layer). Spread preserves evenly over batter; sprinkle chocolate chips over top. Drop reserved batter by $^1/_2$ teaspoons over chips.

4. Bake 25 minutes or until golden. Cool completely in pan on wire rack. Cut into bars.

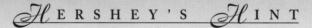

HERSHEY'S HINT

Semi-sweet chocolate is pure chocolate combined with sugar and extra cocoa butter. It is interchangeable with bittersweet chocolate in most recipes.

123

Chocolate Chips and Raspberry Bars

Cherry Cream Filling
(page 126)

½ **cup (1 stick) butter or margarine, melted**

⅓ **cup HERSHEY'S Cocoa**

2 **eggs**

1 **cup sugar**

1 **teaspoon vanilla extract**

½ **cup all-purpose flour**

½ **teaspoon baking powder**

¼ **teaspoon salt**

MARBLED CHERRY BROWNIES

Makes about 16 brownies

1. Prepare Cherry Cream Filling; set aside. Heat oven to 350°F. Grease 9-inch square baking pan.

2. Stir butter and cocoa in small bowl until well blended. Beat eggs in medium bowl until foamy. Gradually add sugar and vanilla, beating until well blended. Stir together flour, baking powder and salt; add to egg mixture. Add cocoa mixture; stir until well blended.

3. Spread half of chocolate batter into prepared pan; cover with cherry filling. Drop teaspoons of remaining chocolate batter over filling. With knife or spatula, gently swirl chocolate batter into filling for marbled effect.

4. Bake 35 to 40 minutes or until brownies begin to pull away from sides of pan. Cool; cut into squares. Cover; refrigerate leftover brownies. Bring to room temperature to serve. *continued on page 126*

Marbled Cherry Brownies

Marbled Cherry Brownies, continued

CHERRY CREAM FILLING

Makes about 1 cup

    1 package (3 ounces) cream cheese, softened

    ¼ cup sugar

    1 egg

    ½ teaspoon vanilla extract

    ¼ teaspoon almond extract

    ⅓ cup chopped maraschino cherries, well drained

    1 to 2 drops red food color (optional)

1. Beat cream cheese and sugar in small bowl on medium speed of mixer until blended. Add egg, vanilla and almond extract; beat well. (Mixture will be thin.)

2. Stir in cherries and food color, if desired.

Prep Time: 25 minutes
Bake Time: 35 minutes
Cool Time: 1¹/₂ hours

*H*ERSHEY'S *H*INT

Store bar cookies and brownies in a tightly covered container or leave them in the pan and cover tightly with aluminum foil.

Chocolate Crust
(recipe follows)

3 packages (8 ounces each)
cream cheese, softened

1 can (14 ounces) sweetened
condensed milk (not
evaporated milk)

3 eggs

2 teaspoons vanilla extract

2 bars (1 ounce each)
HERSHEY'S Unsweetened
Baking Chocolate, melted

MARBLED CHEESECAKE BARS
Makes 24 to 36 bars

1. Prepare Chocolate Crust. Heat oven to 300°F.

2. Beat cream cheese in large bowl until fluffy. Gradually add sweetened condensed milk, beating until smooth. Add eggs and vanilla; mix well.

3. Pour half of batter evenly over prepared crust. Stir melted chocolate into remaining batter; drop by teaspoons over vanilla batter. With metal spatula or knife, swirl gently through batter to marble.

4. Bake 45 to 50 minutes or until set. Cool in pan on wire rack. Refrigerate several hours until chilled. Cut into bars. Cover; store leftover bars in refrigerator.

CHOCOLATE CRUST: Stir together 2 cups vanilla wafer crumbs (about 60 wafers), $1/3$ cup HERSHEY'S Cocoa and $1/2$ cup powdered sugar. Stir in $1/2$ cup (1 stick) melted butter or margarine until well blended. Press mixture firmly onto bottom of ungreased 13×9×2-inch baking pan.

Prep Time: 25 minutes
Bake Time: 45 minutes
Cool Time: 1 hour
Chill Time: $2^1/2$ hours

127

2⅓ cups all-purpose flour

⅔ cup packed light brown
    sugar

¾ cup (1½ sticks) butter or
    margarine

1 egg, slightly beaten

2 cups (12-ounce package)
    HERSHEY'S Semi-Sweet
    Chocolate Chips, divided

1 cup coarsely chopped nuts

1 can (14 ounces) sweetened
    condensed milk (not
    evaporated milk)

1¾ cups (10-ounce package)
    SKOR English Toffee Bits,
    divided

RICH CHOCOLATE CHIP TOFFEE BARS

Makes about 36 bars

1. Heat oven to 350°F. Grease 13×9×2-inch baking pan.

2. Stir together flour and brown sugar in large bowl. Cut in butter with pastry blender or two knives until mixture resembles coarse crumbs. Add egg; mix well. Stir in $1^1/_2$ cups chocolate chips and nuts. Reserve $1^1/_2$ cups mixture. Press remaining crumb mixture onto bottom of prepared pan.

3. Bake 10 minutes. Pour sweetened condensed milk evenly over hot crust. Top with $1^1/_2$ cups toffee bits. Sprinkle reserved crumb mixture and remaining $^1/_2$ cup chips over top.

4. Bake 25 to 30 minutes or until golden brown. Sprinkle with remaining $^1/_4$ cup toffee bits. Cool completely in pan on wire rack. Cut into bars.

Rich Chocolate Chip Toffee Bars

Nut Cream Filling
(recipe follows)

½ cup (1 stick) butter or
  margarine

⅓ cup HERSHEY'S Cocoa

2 eggs

1 cup sugar

1 teaspoon vanilla extract

½ cup all-purpose flour

½ teaspoon baking powder

¼ teaspoon salt

MARBLED BROWNIES

Makes about 20 brownies

1. Prepare Nut Cream Filling; set aside. Heat oven to 350°F. Grease 9-inch square baking pan.

2. Melt butter in small saucepan; remove from heat. Blend in cocoa; set aside to cool slightly. In medium bowl, beat eggs until foamy. Gradually add sugar and vanilla; blend well. Combine flour, baking powder and salt; blend into egg mixture. Stir in chocolate mixture. Remove $3/4$ cup batter; set aside. Spread remaining batter into prepared pan. Spread Nut Cream Filling over batter. Drop teaspoons of reserved batter over top. Swirl gently with metal spatula or knife to marble.

3. Bake 35 to 40 minutes or until brownies begin to pull away from sides of pan. Cool completely on wire rack. Cut into squares.

Nut Cream Filling

1 package (3 ounces) cream cheese, softened

2 tablespoons butter or margarine, softened

¼ cup sugar

1 egg

½ teaspoon vanilla extract

¼ to ½ teaspoon almond extract

1 tablespoon all-purpose flour

¼ cup slivered almonds, toasted* and chopped

To toast almonds, place in shallow baking pan in 350°F oven, stirring occasionally, 8 to 10 minutes or until golden brown. Cool.

Beat cream cheese, butter and sugar in small bowl until creamy. Beat in egg, vanilla and almond extract. Stir in flour and almonds.

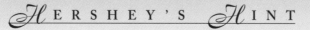

Hershey's Hint

Cool brownies and bars completely before cutting them into squares, rectangles, triangles or other shapes unless the recipe specifies differently. This helps prevent the bars from breaking.

¾ cup HERSHEY'S Cocoa

½ teaspoon baking soda

⅔ cup butter or margarine, melted and divided

½ cup boiling water

2 cups sugar

2 eggs

1⅓ cups all-purpose flour

1 teaspoon vanilla extract

¼ teaspoon salt

¾ cup (3½-ounce jar) macadamia nuts, coarsely chopped

2 cups (12-ounce package) HERSHEY'S Semi-Sweet Chocolate Chips, divided

Vanilla Glaze (recipe follows)

Ultimate Designer Brownies

Makes about 24 brownies

1. Heat oven to 350°F. Grease 13×9-inch baking pan or two 8-inch square baking pans.

2. Stir together cocoa and baking soda in medium bowl; blend in ⅓ cup melted butter. Add boiling water; stir until mixture thickens. Stir in sugar, eggs and remaining ⅓ cup melted butter; stir until smooth. Add flour, vanilla and salt; blend well. Stir in nuts and 1½ cups chocolate chips. Pour into prepared pan(s).

3. Bake 35 to 40 minutes for rectangular pan or 30 to 35 minutes for square pans or until brownies begin to pull away from sides of pan. Cool completely.

4. Prepare Vanilla Glaze; spread on top of cooled brownies. Cut into triangles. Place remaining ½ cup chips in top of double boiler over hot, not boiling, water; stir until melted. Place melted chips in pastry bag fitted with small writing tip; pipe signature design on each brownie.

Vanilla Glaze

Makes about 1 cup

1 tablespoons butter or margarine, softened

1½ cups powdered sugar

1 teaspoon vanilla extract

1 to 2 tablespoons warm water

Combine butter, powdered sugar and vanilla in small bowl; stir in water, a teaspoon at a time, until smooth and of desired consistency.

Ultimate Designer Brownie

3¾ cups (10-ounce package)
    MOUNDS Sweetened
    Coconut Flakes

¾ cup sugar

¼ cup all-purpose flour

¼ teaspoon salt

3 egg whites

1 whole egg, slightly beaten

1 teaspoon almond extract

1 cup HERSHEY'S MINI KISSES
    Milk Chocolate Baking
    Pieces

MINI KISSES COCONUT MACAROON BARS

Makes about 24 bars

1. Heat oven to 350°F. Lightly grease 9-inch square baking pan.

2. Stir together coconut, sugar, flour and salt in large bowl. Add egg whites, whole egg and almond extract; stir until well blended. Stir in Mini Kisses. Spread mixture into prepared pan, covering all chocolate pieces with coconut mixture.

3. Bake 35 minutes or until lightly browned. Cool completely in pan on wire rack. Cover with foil; allow to stand at room temperature about 8 hours or overnight. Cut into bars.

VARIATION: Omit Mini Kisses in batter. Immediately after removing pan from oven, place desired number of chocolate pieces on top, pressing down lightly. Cool completely. Cut into bars.

Prep Time: 15 minutes
Bake Time: 35 minutes
Cool Time: 8 hours

Mini Kisses Coconut Macaroon Bars

¾ cup HERSHEY'S Cocoa

½ teaspoon baking soda

⅔ cup butter or margarine, melted and divided

½ cup boiling water

2 cups sugar

2 eggs

1⅓ cups all-purpose flour

1 teaspoon vanilla extract

¼ teaspoon salt

1⅔ cups (10-ounce package) HERSHEY'S Mint Chocolate Chips

Glaze (recipe follows, optional)

HERSHEY'S CHOCOLATE MINT BROWNIES

Makes about 36 brownies

1. Heat oven to 350°F. Grease 13×9×2-inch baking pan.

2. Stir together cocoa and baking soda in large bowl; stir in $^1/_3$ cup butter. Add boiling water; stir until mixture thickens. Stir in sugar, eggs and remaining $^1/_3$ cup butter; stir until smooth. Add flour, vanilla and salt; stir until well blended. Stir in mint chocolate chips. Spread batter into prepared pan.

3. Bake 35 to 40 minutes or until brownies begin to pull away from sides of pan. Cool completely in pan on wire rack. Prepare glaze; drizzle over tops of brownies, if desired. Cut into bars.

GLAZE: In small bowl, combine $^2/_3$ cup powdered sugar and 2 to 3 teaspoons milk; stir in few drops green food color, if desired.

1 ⅓ cups all-purpose flour

2 tablespoons plus ½ cup packed light brown sugar, divided

½ cup (1 stick) cold butter or margarine

2 eggs

½ cup light corn syrup

¼ cup HERSHEY'S Cocoa

2 tablespoons butter or margarine, melted

1 teaspoon vanilla extract

⅛ teaspoon salt

1 cup coarsely chopped pecans

CHOCOLATE PECAN PIE BARS

Makes about 16 bars

1. Heat oven to 350°F.

2. Stir together flour and 2 tablespoons brown sugar in large bowl. Cut in ½ cup butter with pastry blender or two knives until mixture resembles coarse crumbs; press onto bottom and about 1 inch up sides of ungreased 9-inch square baking pan.

3. Bake 10 to 12 minutes or until set. Remove from oven. With back of spoon, lightly press crust into corners and against sides of pan. Meanwhile, lightly beat eggs, corn syrup, remaining ½ cup brown sugar, cocoa, melted butter, vanilla and salt in medium bowl. Stir in pecans. Pour mixture over warm crust. Return to oven.

4. Bake 25 minutes or until pecan filling is set. Cool completely in pan on wire rack. Cut into bars.

1 cup (2 sticks) butter or margarine, softened

2 cups packed light brown sugar

2 eggs

1 teaspoon vanilla extract

½ teaspoon powdered instant coffee (optional)

3 cups quick-cooking oats

2½ cups all-purpose flour

1 teaspoon baking soda

½ teaspoon salt

1½ cups chopped walnuts, divided

Chocolate Filling (recipe follows)

FUDGE FILLED WALNUT-OATMEAL BARS

Makes about 48 bars

1. Heat oven to 350°F. Beat butter and brown sugar in large bowl until creamy. Add eggs, vanilla and instant coffee, if desired; beat well. Stir together oats, flour, baking soda, salt and 1 cup walnuts; gradually add to butter mixture, beating until well blended. (Batter will be stiff; stir in last part by hand.)

3. Remove 2 cups batter. Press remaining dough onto bottom of 15½×10½×1-inch jelly-roll pan. Prepare Chocolate Filling; spread over mixture in pan. Sprinkle reserved dough over filling. Sprinkle with remaining ½ cup walnuts.

4. Bake 25 minutes or until top is golden. (Chocolate will be soft.) Cool completely in pan on wire rack. Cut into bars.

CHOCOLATE FILLING

1 tablespoon butter or margarine

3½ bars (1 ounce each) HERSHEY'S Unsweetened Baking Chocolate, broken into pieces

½ cup sugar

1 can (14 ounces) sweetened condensed milk (not evaporated milk)

1½ teaspoons vanilla extract

Melt butter in medium saucepan over low heat. Add chocolate; cook until smooth and completely melted, stirring occasionally. Stir in sugar and sweetened condensed milk. Cook, stirring constantly, until mixture thickens and sugar is dissolved. Remove from heat. Stir in vanilla.

Fudge Filled Walnut–Oatmeal Bars

1 cup (2 sticks) butter or margarine, softened

1 package (3 ounces) cream cheese, softened

2 cups sugar

3 eggs

1 teaspoon vanilla extract

1 cup all-purpose flour

¾ cup HERSHEY'S Cocoa

½ teaspoon salt

¼ teaspoon baking powder

1⅔ cups (10-ounce package) REESE'S Peanut Butter Chips

Brownie Frosting (recipe follows, optional)

IRRESISTIBLE PEANUT BUTTER CHIP BROWNIES

Makes about 36 bars

1. Heat oven to 325°F. Grease bottom of 13×9×2-inch baking pan.

2. Beat butter, cream cheese and sugar until fluffy. Beat in eggs and vanilla. Combine flour, cocoa, salt and baking powder; gradually add to butter mixture, beating well. Stir in chips. Spread batter into pan.

3. Bake 35 to 40 minutes or until brownies begin to pull away from sides of pan. Cool completely. Frost with Brownie Frosting, if desired. Cut into bars.

BROWNIE FROSTING: Beat 3 tablespoons softened butter or margarine and 3 tablespoons HERSHEY'S Cocoa until blended. Gradually add 1⅓ cups powdered sugar and ¾ teaspoon vanilla extract alternately with 1 to 2 tablespoons milk, beating to spreading consistency. Makes about 1 cup frosting.

2 cups all-purpose flour

1 cup packed light brown sugar

½ cup (1 stick) butter

1 cup pecan halves

Toffee Topping (recipe follows)

1 cup HERSHEY'S Milk Chocolate Chips

ENGLISH TOFFEE BARS

Makes about 36 bars

1. Heat oven to 350°F.

2. Combine flour, brown sugar and butter in large bowl; mix until fine crumbs form (a few large crumbs may remain). Press into ungreased 13×9-inch baking pan. Sprinkle pecans over crust. Prepare Toffee Topping; drizzle evenly over pecans and crust.

3. Bake 20 to 22 minutes or until topping is bubbly and golden. Remove from oven. Immediately sprinkle chocolate chips over top; press gently onto surface. Cool completely. Cut into bars.

TOFFEE TOPPING: In small saucepan, combine ⅔ cup butter and ⅓ cup packed light brown sugar. Cook over medium heat, stirring constantly, until mixture comes to boil; boil and stir 30 seconds. Use immediately.

1 cup (2 sticks) butter or
   margarine

2 cups sugar

2 teaspoons vanilla extract

4 eggs

¾ cup HERSHEY'S Cocoa *or*
   HERSHEY'S Dutch
   Processed Cocoa

1¾ cups all-purpose flour

½ teaspoon baking powder

½ teaspoon salt

1⅔ cups (10-ounce package)
   REESE'S Peanut Butter
   Chips, divided

P.B. Chips Brownie Cups

Makes about 18 brownie cups

1. Heat oven to 350°F. Line 18 muffin cups (2½ inches in diameter) with paper or foil baking cups.

2. Place butter in large microwave-safe bowl. Microwave at HIGH (100%) 1 to 1½ minutes or until melted. Stir in sugar and vanilla. Add eggs; beat well. Add cocoa; beat until well blended. Add flour, baking powder and salt; beat well. Stir in 1⅓ cups peanut butter chips. Divide batter evenly into muffin cups; sprinkle with remaining ⅓ cup peanut butter chips.

3. Bake 25 to 30 minutes or until surface is firm; cool completely in pan on wire rack.

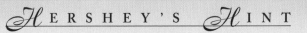

Hershey's Hint

Butter and margarine are interchangeable if they are both listed in the ingredient list. Do not use low-fat spreads or soft or tub margarines unless the recipe specifically calls for these ingredients. They act differently and may cause unsatisfactory results.

P.B. Chips Brownie Cups

¾ cup HERSHEY'S Cocoa

½ teaspoon baking soda

⅔ cup butter or margarine,
   melted and divided

½ cup boiling water

2 cups sugar

2 eggs

1⅓ cups all-purpose flour

1 teaspoon vanilla extract

¼ teaspoon salt

1 cup HERSHEY'S Semi-Sweet
   Chocolate Chips

One-Bowl Buttercream
   Frosting (recipe follows)

ULTIMATE CHOCOLATE BROWNIES

Makes about 36 brownies

1. Heat oven to 350°F. Grease 13×9×2-inch baking pan or two 8-inch square baking pans.

2. Stir together cocoa and baking soda in large bowl; stir in ⅓ cup butter. Add boiling water; stir until mixture thickens. Stir in sugar, eggs and remaining ⅓ cup butter; stir until smooth. Add flour, vanilla and salt; blend completely. Stir in chocolate chips. Pour into prepared pan(s).

3. Bake 35 to 40 minutes for rectangular pan, 30 to 35 minutes for square pans or until brownies begin to pull away from sides of pans. Cool completely in pans on wire rack. Meanwhile, prepare One-Bowl Buttercream Frosting; frost brownies. Sprinkle with additional chocolate chips, if desired. Cut into squares.

ONE-BOWL BUTTERCREAM FROSTING

6 tablespoons butter or margarine, softened

2⅔ cups powdered sugar

½ cup HERSHEY'S Cocoa *or* HERSHEY'S Dutch
   Processed Cocoa

4 to 6 tablespoons milk

1 teaspoon vanilla extract

Beat butter in medium bowl. Add powdered sugar and cocoa alternately with milk, beating to spreading consistency. Stir in vanilla.

Ultimate Chocolate Brownies

½ cup (1 stick) butter or
    margarine, softened

1 cup sugar

2 eggs

1½ teaspoons vanilla extract

1½ cups all-purpose flour

1 teaspoon baking powder

½ teaspoon baking soda

¼ teaspoon salt

¼ cup HERSHEY'S Cocoa

½ cup canned pumpkin

½ teaspoon pumpkin pie spice

Chocolate Frosting (recipe
    follows)

CHOCOLATE AND PUMPKIN SQUARES

Makes about 16 squares

1. Heat oven to 350°F. Grease 9-inch square baking pan.

2. Beat butter and sugar in medium bowl until well blended. Add eggs and vanilla; beat until smooth and creamy. Stir together flour, baking powder, baking soda and salt; gradually add to butter mixture. Remove 1¼ cups batter to small bowl; add cocoa, blending well. To remaining batter, blend in pumpkin and pumpkin pie spice. Spread chocolate batter into prepared pan; spread pumpkin batter over chocolate.

3. Bake 30 minutes or until brownies begin to pull away from sides of pan. Cool completely in pan on wire rack. Prepare Chocolate Frosting; frost. Cut into squares.

CHOCOLATE FROSTING

Makes about 1 cup

1 cup powdered sugar

¼ cup HERSHEY'S Cocoa

3 tablespoons butter or margarine, softened

2 to 3 tablespoons milk

½ teaspoon vanilla extract

Stir together powdered sugar and cocoa. Beat butter in small bowl until creamy; gradually add sugar mixture alternately with milk, beating until desired consistency. Stir in vanilla.

1 cup (2 sticks) butter or margarine, softened

1 package (3 ounces) cream cheese, softened

2 cups sugar

3 eggs

1 teaspoon vanilla extract

1 cup all-purpose flour

¾ cup HERSHEY'S Cocoa

¼ teaspoon baking powder

½ teaspoon salt

¾ cup chopped nuts

Brownie Frosting (recipe follows)

CHOCOLATE CREAM CHEESE BROWNIES

Makes about 36 brownies

1. Heat oven to 325°F. Grease bottom of 13×9×2-inch baking pan.

2. Beat butter, cream cheese and sugar in large bowl until fluffy. Add eggs and vanilla; beat well. Stir together flour, cocoa, baking powder and salt; gradually add to butter mixture, blending well. Stir in nuts. Spread batter into prepared pan.

3. Bake 35 to 40 minutes or just until brownies begin to pull away from sides of pan. Cool completely in pan on wire rack. Prepare Brownie Frosting; spread over brownies. Cut into bars.

BROWNIE FROSTING

Makes about 1 cup frosting

3 tablespoons butter or margarine, softened

3 tablespoons HERSHEY'S Cocoa

1⅓ cups powdered sugar

¾ teaspoon vanilla extract

1 tablespoon milk

1 tablespoon light corn syrup (optional)

Beat butter and cocoa in small bowl until blended; gradually add powdered sugar and vanilla, beating well. Add milk and corn syrup, if desired; beat until smooth and of spreading consistency. Add additional milk, $1/2$ teaspoon at a time, if needed.

147

2 cups all-purpose flour

1⅓ cups packed light brown sugar, divided

½ cup (1 stick) plus ⅔ cup butter, divided

1 cup coarsely chopped pecans

1¾ cups (10-ounce package) HERSHEY'S MINI KISSES Chocolate Baking Pieces

MINI KISSES PRALINE BARS

Makes about 36 bars

1. Heat oven to 350°F.

2. Stir together flour and 1 cup brown sugar in large bowl; cut in ½ cup butter with pastry blender or two knives until fine crumbs form. Press mixture into 13×9×2-inch baking pan; sprinkle with pecans.

3. Place remaining ⅔ cup butter and remaining ⅓ cup brown sugar in small saucepan; cook over medium heat, stirring constantly, until mixture boils. Continue boiling, stirring constantly, 30 seconds, until sugar dissolves; drizzle evenly over pecans and crust.

4. Bake 18 to 22 minutes until topping is bubbly and golden; remove from oven. Immediately sprinkle Mini Kisses over top. Cool completely in pan on wire rack. Cut into bars.

Mini Kisses Praline Bars

1½ cups finely crushed unsalted pretzels

¾ cup (1½ sticks) butter or margarine, melted

1 can (14 ounces) sweetened condensed milk (not evaporated milk)

2 cups miniature marshmallows

1 cup HERSHEY'S Butterscotch Chips

1 cup HERSHEY'S Semi-Sweet Chocolate Chips

1 cup MOUNDS Sweetened Coconut Flakes

¾ cup chopped nuts

Chewy Rocky Road Bars

Makes about 36 bars

1. Heat oven to 350°F.

2. Combine crushed pretzels and butter in small bowl; lightly press mixture onto bottom of 13×9×2-inch baking pan. Pour sweetened condensed milk evenly over crumb mixture. Top with marshmallows, butterscotch chips, chocolate chips, coconut and nuts. Press toppings firmly into sweetened condensed milk.

3. Bake 25 to 30 minutes or until lightly browned. Cool completely in pan on wire rack. Cut into bars.

Variations: 2 cups (12-ounce package) HERSHEY'S Semi-Sweet Chocolate Chips or 1²/₃ cups (10-ounce package) HERSHEY'S Butterscotch Chips may be used instead of 1 cup of each flavor.

¾ cup (1½ sticks) butter or margarine

1¾ cups graham cracker crumbs

¼ cup HERSHEY'S Cocoa

2 tablespoons sugar

1 can (14 ounces) sweetened condensed milk (not evaporated milk)

1 cup HERSHEY'S Semi-Sweet Chocolate Chips

1 cup raisins, chopped dried apricots or miniature marshmallows

1 cup chopped nuts

FIVE LAYER BARS

Makes about 36 bars

1. Heat oven to 350°F. Place butter in 13×9×2-inch baking pan. Heat in oven until melted. Remove pan from oven.

2. Stir together graham cracker crumbs, cocoa and sugar; sprinkle evenly over butter. Pour sweetened condensed milk evenly over crumb mixture. Sprinkle with chocolate chips and raisins. Sprinkle nuts on top; press down firmly.

3. Bake 25 to 30 minutes or until lightly browned. Cool completely in pan on wire rack. Cover with foil; let stand at room temperature 6 to 8 hours. Cut into bars.

VARIATION: Substitute 1 cup REESE'S Peanut Butter Chips for chocolate chips. Proceed as directed above.

DESSERT CREATIONS

1 envelope unflavored gelatin

2 tablespoons cold water

¼ cup boiling water

1 cup sugar

½ cup HERSHEY'S Cocoa

2 cups (1 pint) cold whipping cream

2 teaspoons vanilla extract

Fresh raspberries or sliced strawberries

SWEETHEART CHOCOLATE MOUSSE

Makes about 8 servings

1. Sprinkle gelatin over cold water in small bowl; let stand 2 minutes to soften. Add boiling water; stir until gelatin is completely dissolved and mixture is clear. Cool slightly.

2. Mix sugar and cocoa in large bowl; add whipping cream and vanilla. Beat on medium speed of mixer, scraping bottom of bowl occasionally, until mixture is stiff. Pour in gelatin mixture; beat until well blended.

3. Spoon into dessert dishes. Refrigerate at least 30 minutes before serving. Garnish with fruit.

153

Sweetheart Chocolate Mousse

½ cup water

¼ cup (½ stick) butter or
    margarine

⅛ teaspoon salt

½ cup all-purpose flour

2 eggs

    Chocolate Mousse Filling
      (page 156)

    Chocolate Glaze (page 156)
      or powdered sugar

CHOCOLATE MINI-PUFFS

Makes about 2 to 2½ dozen mini-puffs

1. Heat oven to 400°F.

2. Combine water, butter and salt in medium saucepan. Cook over medium heat, stirring constantly, until mixture comes to full rolling boil; turn heat to low.

3. Add flour all at once; cook over low heat, stirring vigorously, until mixture leaves side of pan and forms a ball, about 1 minute. Remove from heat; cool slightly. Add eggs, one at a time, beating with wooden spoon until smooth and velvety. Drop by scant teaspoons onto ungreased cookie sheet.

4. Bake 25 to 30 minutes or until puffed and golden brown. Remove from oven; cool on wire racks.

5. Prepare Chocolate Mousse Filling. Slice off tops of puffs. With spoon, fill puffs with filling or pipe filling into puffs using a pastry bag fitted with $1/4$-inch tip. Replace tops and sprinkle with powdered sugar or prepare Chocolate Glaze; drizzle onto puffs. Refrigerate until serving time.

continued on page 156

154

Chocolate Mini-Puffs

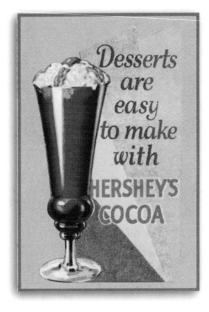

Chocolate Mini-Puffs, continued

CHOCOLATE MOUSSE FILLING

Makes about 2 cups filling

- 1 teaspoon unflavored gelatin
- 1 tablespoon cold water
- 2 tablespoons boiling water
- ½ cup sugar
- ¼ cup HERSHEY'S Cocoa
- 1 cup (½ pint) cold whipping cream
- 1 teaspoon vanilla extract

1. Sprinkle gelatin over cold water in small bowl; let stand 1 minute to soften. Add boiling water; stir until gelatin is completely dissolved and mixture is clear. Cool slightly.

2. Stir together sugar and cocoa in medium bowl; add whipping cream and vanilla. Beat at medium speed, scraping bottom of bowl occasionally, until stiff; pour in gelatin mixture and beat until well blended. Refrigerate ¹/₂ hour.

CHOCOLATE GLAZE: Melt 2 tablespoons butter or margarine in small saucepan over low heat; add 2 tablespoons HERSHEY'S Cocoa and 2 tablespoons water. Cook and stir over low heat until smooth and slightly thickened; do not boil. Remove from heat; cool slightly.

1 envelope unflavored gelatin

2 tablespoons cold water

2 tablespoons boiling water

1 cup strawberry yogurt

1 package (10 ounces) frozen strawberries, thawed and puréed

½ cup cold whipping cream

⅓ cup sugar

3 tablespoons HERSHEY'S Cocoa

1 teaspoon vanilla extract

¼ cup slivered almonds

¼ cup granola-type cereal

FROZEN COCO-BERRY YOGURT SUPREME

Makes about 6 servings

1. Sprinkle gelatin over cold water in small bowl; let stand 1 minute to soften. Add boiling water; stir until gelatin is completely dissolved and mixture is clear.

2. Stir together yogurt, strawberries, whipping cream, sugar, cocoa and vanilla in medium bowl. Add gelatin mixture; blend thoroughly.

3. Pour mixture into 8-inch square pan; freeze until thickened. Remove mixture from pan to small bowl; beat until ice crystals are broken. Fold in almonds and granola. Return mixture to pan; cover and freeze until firm. Allow to soften at room temperature 5 minutes before serving.

¾ cup sugar

¼ cup HERSHEY'S Cocoa

1½ cups (12-ounce can) evaporated nonfat milk

¼ teaspoon mint extract

COCOA MINT SHERBET

Makes 6 servings (¼ cup each)

Stir together sugar and cocoa in medium saucepan; add evaporated milk. Cook over medium heat, stirring constantly, until sugar dissolves and mixture is smooth. Remove from heat; stir in mint extract. Pour into 8-inch square pan. Place in freezer, stirring occasionally, until frozen.

2 medium-size ripe bananas

1 cup apricot nectar or peach or pineapple juice, divided

½ cup HERSHEY'S Semi-Sweet Chocolate Chips

2 tablespoons sugar

1 cup milk

CHOCOLATE-BANANA SHERBET

Makes about 8 servings (3¼ cups)

1. Slice bananas into blender container or food processor. Add ³/₄ cup fruit juice. Cover; blend until smooth.

2. Place chocolate chips, remaining ¹/₄ cup fruit juice and sugar in small microwave-safe bowl. Microwave at HIGH (100%) 30 seconds; stir. If necessary, microwave at HIGH an additional 15 seconds at a time, stirring after each heating, just until chips are melted and mixture is smooth when stirred.

3. Add to mixture in blender. Cover; blend until thoroughly combined. Add milk. Cover; blend until smooth. Pour into 9-inch square pan. Cover; freeze until hard around edges, about 2 hours.

4. Spoon partially frozen mixture into large bowl or food processor; beat until smooth but not melted. Return mixture to pan. Cover; freeze until firm, stirring several times before mixture freezes. Allow to soften at room temperature 5 to 10 minutes before serving. Scoop into dessert dishes.

Chocolate-Banana Sherbet

4 eggs, separated and at room temperature

½ cup plus ⅓ cup sugar, divided

1 teaspoon vanilla extract

½ cup all-purpose flour

⅓ cup HERSHEY'S Cocoa

½ teaspoon baking powder

¼ teaspoon baking soda

⅛ teaspoon salt

⅓ cup water

Chocolate Peach Filling (page 163)

Peach Melba Topping (page 162)

Peach slices, fresh* or canned

*To keep fresh peaches from turning brown, dip in mixture of 1 cup water, ½ teaspoon lemon juice and ⅛ teaspoon salt; drain well before placing on top of dessert.

CHOCOLATE PEACH CHARLOTTE WITH PEACH MELBA TOPPING

Makes 12 to 14 servings

1. Heat oven to 375°F. Line 15½×10½×1-inch jelly-roll pan with foil; generously grease foil.

2. Beat egg whites in large bowl until soft peaks form; gradually add ½ cup sugar, beating until stiff peaks form. Beat egg yolks and vanilla in small bowl on high speed of mixer about 3 minutes; gradually add remaining ⅓ cup sugar. Continue beating 2 additional minutes.

3. Stir together flour, cocoa, baking powder, baking soda and salt; on low speed, add to egg yolk mixture alternately with water, beating just until batter is smooth. Gradually fold chocolate mixture into egg whites; spread evenly in prepared pan.

4. Bake 12 to 15 minutes or until top springs back when touched lightly in center. Immediately loosen cake from edges of pan. Place foil over cake; invert cake onto countertop. Remove pan; allow to cool. Prepare Chocolate Peach Filling.

5. Peel foil off cake. When completely cool, cut a circle from one end of cake to fit bottom of 9-inch springform pan. Divide remaining cake into 3 equal vertical strips. Cut across strips forming sticks approximately 3×1 inches. Place sticks vertically around inside edge of springform pan; pour filling into cake-lined pan. Refrigerate 4 to 6 hours or until firm. *continued on page 162*

Chocolate Peach Charlotte with Peach Melba Topping

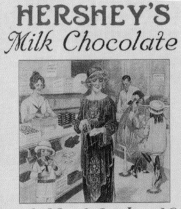

HERSHEY'S Milk Chocolate

A Meal In Itself

MADE IN HERSHEY, PA., THE CHOCOLATE AND COCOA TOWN"

Chocolate Peach Charlotte with Peach Melba Topping, continued

6. Make Peach Melba Topping. To serve, remove side of springform pan. Spoon on topping. Arrange peach slices on top. Cover; refrigerate.

CHOCOLATE PEACH FILLING

  2 envelopes unflavored gelatin
  ¾ cup cold water
  1 cup sugar
  ⅓ cup HERSHEY'S Cocoa
  ¼ cup (½ stick) butter or margarine
2¼ cups milk, divided
  1 teaspoon vanilla extract
  1 cup (½ pint) cold whipping cream
  1 cup puréed peaches, fresh or canned

1. Sprinkle gelatin over water in small bowl; let stand 3 or 4 minutes to soften. Combine sugar, cocoa, butter and $1/2$ cup milk in medium saucepan; cook over low heat, stirring constantly, until mixture is smooth and very hot. Do not boil. Add gelatin mixture, stirring until gelatin is completely dissolved.

2. Remove from heat; gradually add remaining $1^3/_4$ cups milk and vanilla. Pour into bowl; refrigerate, stirring occasionally, until mixture mounds when dropped from a spoon.

3. Beat whipping cream in medium bowl until stiff; fold with puréed peaches into chocolate mixture.

PEACH MELBA TOPPING: Stir together $1/3$ cup seedless red raspberry preserves and $1/4$ teaspoon lemon juice in small saucepan. Mix 1 teaspoon cornstarch with 2 tablespoons water; add to raspberry mixture. Cook over medium heat, stirring constantly, until mixture begins to boil and thickens slightly; remove from heat. Stir in $1/4$ teaspoon almond extract. Cool.

CHOCOLATE CHERRY-ALMOND ICE CREAM

Makes $2^{1}/2$ quarts ice cream

6 egg yolks

6 cups light cream, divided

2 cups sugar

$2/3$ cup HERSHEY'S Cocoa

1 cup coarsely chopped
 almonds, toasted*

1 teaspoon almond extract

1 cup chopped maraschino
 cherries, drained

To toast almonds, heat oven to 350°F. Spread almonds in thin layer in shallow baking pan. Bake 8 to 10 minutes, stirring occasionally, until light golden brown; cool.

1. Beat egg yolks and 2 cups cream in large bowl; set aside.

2. Stir together sugar and cocoa in large saucepan; gradually stir in egg yolk mixture. Cook over medium heat, stirring constantly, until mixture is very hot; do not boil. Remove from heat; cool to room temperature. Meanwhile, coarsely chop almonds; set aside.

3. Stir remaining 4 cups cream and almond extract into chocolate mixture, blending well. Chill mixture at least 6 hours; pour into cylinder of 5-quart ice cream freezer. Freeze according to manufacturer's directions; immediately fold in cherries and almonds. To ripen, repack in ice and salt; let stand several hours.

163

1 envelope unflavored gelatin

½ cup cold water

⅓ cup sugar

3 tablespoons HERSHEY'S Cocoa

1½ cups low-fat (1%) milk

2 egg yolks, slightly beaten

2 teaspoons vanilla extract

1 cup frozen light non-dairy whipped topping, thawed

Additional whipped topping

Fresh raspberries or canned fruit slices, drained

CHOCOLATE DESSERT TIMBALES

Makes 6 servings

1. Sprinkle gelatin over cold water in small bowl; let stand several minutes to soften.

2. Stir together sugar and cocoa in medium saucepan; gradually stir in milk. Stir in egg yolks. Cook over medium heat, stirring constantly, until mixture just begins to boil; remove from heat. Stir in reserved gelatin mixture and vanilla; stir until gelatin is completely dissolved. Transfer to medium bowl; refrigerate, stirring occasionally, until mixture begins to set.

3. Carefully fold 1 cup whipped topping into chocolate mixture, blending until smooth. Pour into 6 small serving dishes or custard cups; refrigerate until set. Garnish with additional whipped topping and fruit.

Chocolate Dessert Timbales

3 eggs

¾ cup water

½ cup light cream or half-and-half

¾ cup plus 2 tablespoons all-purpose flour

3 tablespoons HERSHEY'S Cocoa

2 tablespoons sugar

⅛ teaspoon salt

3 tablespoons butter or margarine, melted and cooled

Cherry pie filling

Chocolate Sauce (recipe follows)

Sweetened whipped cream (optional)

COCOA BLACK FOREST CRÊPES

Makes about 18 crêpes

1. Combine eggs, water and light cream in blender or food processor; blend 10 seconds. Add flour, cocoa, sugar, salt and butter; blend until smooth. Let stand at room temperature 30 minutes.

2. Spray 6-inch crêpe pan lightly with vegetable cooking spray; heat over medium heat. For each crêpe, pour 2 to 3 tablespoons batter into pan; lift and tilt pan to spread batter. Return to heat; cook until surface begins to dry. Loosen crêpe around edges; turn and lightly cook other side. Stack crêpes, placing wax paper between crêpes. Keep covered. (Refrigerate for later use, if desired.)

3. Just before serving, place 2 tablespoons pie filling onto each crêpe; roll up. Place crêpes on dessert plate. Prepare Chocolate Sauce; spoon over crêpes. Garnish with sweetened whipped cream, if desired.

CHOCOLATE SAUCE: Stir together ³/₄ cup sugar and ¹/₃ cup HERSHEY'S Cocoa in small saucepan; blend in ³/₄ cup evaporated milk, ¹/₄ cup butter and ¹/₈ teaspoon salt. Cook over medium heat, stirring constantly, until mixture comes to a boil. Remove from heat; stir in 1 teaspoon kirsch (cherry brandy), if desired. Serve warm. Cover; refrigerate leftover sauce.

Top to bottom: Crunchy Nutty Ice Cream Sundae (page 168), Cocoa Black Forest Crêpes

**Peanut Butter Sauce
(recipe follows)**

**Coconut Crunch
(recipe follows)**

1 pint vanilla ice cream

CRUNCHY NUTTY ICE CREAM SUNDAES

Makes 4 sundaes

Prepare Peanut Butter Sauce and Coconut Crunch. Spoon sauce over scoops of ice cream; sprinkle crunch over top. Serve immediately.

PEANUT BUTTER SAUCE: Melt 1 cup REESE'S Peanut Butter Chips with $^1/_3$ cup milk and $^1/_4$ cup whipping cream in medium saucepan over low heat, stirring constantly, until chips are melted. Remove from heat; stir in $^1/_4$ teaspoon vanilla extract. Cool to room temperature. Makes 1 cup sauce.

COCONUT CRUNCH: Heat oven to 325°F. Combine $^1/_2$ cup MOUNDS Sweetened Coconut Flakes, $^1/_2$ cup chopped nuts and 1 tablespoon butter or margarine in shallow baking pan. Toast in oven, stirring occasionally, 6 to 8 minutes or until butter is melted and mixture is very lightly browned. (Watch carefully so mixture does not burn.) Cool to room temperature. Makes about 1 cup.

2 tablespoons sugar

½ teaspoon unflavored gelatin

¼ cup milk

½ cup HERSHEY'S MINI CHIPS
Semi-Sweet Chocolate

1 tablespoon orange-
flavored liqueur, rum or
1 teaspoon vanilla extract

½ cup cold whipping cream

Additional sweetened
whipped cream (optional)

CHOCOLATE LOVER'S MOUSSE FOR TWO

Makes 2 servings

1. Stir together sugar and gelatin in small saucepan; stir in milk. Let stand 2 minutes to soften gelatin. Cook over medium heat, stirring constantly, until mixture begins to boil. Remove from heat. Immediately add Mini Chips; stir until melted. Stir in liqueur; cool to room temperature.

2. Beat whipping cream in small bowl on high speed of mixer until stiff. Gradually fold in chocolate mixture. Spoon into serving dishes. Refrigerate before serving. Garnish with additional sweetened whipped cream, if desired.

NOTE: For high-standing mousse, prepare collars for two parfait glasses. Tear strip of foil of sufficient length to go around top of each glass. Fold foil lengthwise into fourths; butter lightly. Place buttered side in; tape to sides of glasses. Pour mousse into glasses. (Mousse should come over top of glass.) After mousse has set, carefully remove foil collar.

1½ cups HERSHEY'S MINI CHIPS
Semi-Sweet Chocolate *or*
1 HERSHEY'S Milk
Chocolate Bar (7 ounces),
broken into pieces

Peanut Butter Filling
(recipe follows)

24 HERSHEY'S KISSES Milk
Chocolates

CHOCOLATE FLUTED KISS CUPS

Makes about 24 servings

1. Line small muffin cups ($1^3/_4$ inches in diameter) with small paper bake cups.

2. Place Mini Chips in small microwave-safe bowl. Microwave at HIGH (100%) 1 minute; stir. If necessary, microwave at HIGH an additional 15 seconds at a time, stirring after each heating, just until chips are melted when stirred. With small brush, coat insides of paper cups with melted chocolate. Refrigerate 20 minutes; coat any thin spots. Refrigerate until firm, preferably overnight.

3. Gently peel paper from chocolate cups. Prepare Peanut Butter Filling; spoon into cups. Cover; refrigerate before serving. Remove wrappers from chocolate pieces. Before serving, top each cup with chocolate piece.

PEANUT BUTTER FILLING

1 cup REESE'S Creamy Peanut Butter

1 cup powdered sugar

1 tablespoon butter or margarine, softened

Beat peanut butter, powdered sugar and butter in small bowl until smooth.

Chocolate Fluted Kiss Cups

3 tablespoons butter or
　　margarine, melted

2 tablespoons sugar

1 cup graham cracker crumbs

½ cup milk

1 HERSHEY'S Milk Chocolate
　　Bar (7 ounces), broken
　　into pieces

½ cup HERSHEY'S MINI CHIPS
　　Semi-Sweet Chocolate

1 cup (½ pint) cold whipping
　　cream

　　Sweetened whipped cream

　　Sliced strawberries

DOUBLE CHOCOLATE DELIGHT

Makes 6 to 8 servings

1. Stir together butter and sugar in small bowl. Add graham cracker crumbs; mix well. Press mixture firmly onto bottom of 8-inch square pan. Refrigerate 1 to 2 hours or until firm.

2. Meanwhile, heat milk in small saucepan just until it begins to boil; remove from heat. Immediately add chocolate bar pieces and Mini Chips; stir until chocolate melts and mixture is smooth. Pour into medium bowl; cool to room temperature.

3. Beat whipping cream in small bowl on high speed of mixer until stiff; fold gently into chocolate mixture. Pour onto prepared crust; freeze several hours or until firm. Cut into squares. Just before serving, garnish with sweetened whipped cream and strawberries.

HERSHEY'S HINT

White chocolate is not really chocolate at all because it lacks chocolate liquor (the main component in unsweetened chocolate). White chocolate is cocoa butter with added sugar, milk and flavorings (often vanilla or vanillin). It is more delicate than other chocolates and burns easily.

Top to bottom: Classic Chocolate Pudding (page 174), Double Chocolate Delight

2 bars (1 ounce *each*)
HERSHEY'S Unsweetened
Baking Chocolate, broken
into pieces

2½ cups milk, divided

1 cup sugar

¼ cup cornstarch

½ teaspoon salt

3 egg yolks, slightly beaten

1 tablespoon butter (do not
use margarine)

1 teaspoon vanilla extract

Sweetened whipped cream
(optional)

Pecan halves (optional)

CLASSIC CHOCOLATE PUDDING

Makes 4 to 6 servings

1. Combine chocolate and $1^1/_2$ cups milk in medium saucepan; cook over low heat, stirring constantly with whisk, until chocolate is melted and mixture is smooth.

2. Stir together sugar, cornstarch and salt in medium bowl; blend in remaining 1 cup milk and egg yolks. Gradually stir into chocolate mixture. Cook over medium heat, stirring constantly, until mixture comes to a boil. Boil 1 minute, stirring constantly.

3. Remove from heat; add butter and vanilla. Pour into bowl; press plastic wrap directly onto surface. Refrigerate 2 to 3 hours or until cold. Just before serving, garnish with sweetened whipped cream and pecans, if desired.

HERSHEY'S HINT

Pudding is a term that most often describes a creamy cooked dessert made with milk, sugar, flavoring and a thickener, such as eggs, cornstarch or tapioca. Puddings can be homemade or prepared from mixes, which require only the addition of milk. Other types of puddings include baked puddings, such as bread pudding and rice pudding.

1 cup (2 sticks) butter or
　　margarine, melted
1½ cups sugar
1½ teaspoons vanilla extract
　3 eggs, separated and at room
　　temperature
⅔ cup HERSHEY'S Cocoa
½ cup all-purpose flour
　3 tablespoons water
¾ cup finely chopped pecans
⅛ teaspoon cream of tartar
⅛ teaspoon salt
　2 cups (12-ounce package)
　　HERSHEY'S Semi-Sweet
　　Chocolate Chips, divided
　Royal Chip Glaze
　　(recipe follows)
　Sweetened whipped cream
　　(optional)
　Pecan halves (optional)

CHOCOLATE CHIPS PECAN TORTE

Makes 10 to 12 servings

1. Heat oven to 350°F. Line bottom of 9-inch springform pan with foil; butter foil and side of pan.

2. Combine melted butter, sugar and vanilla; beat well. Add egg yolks, one at a time, beating after each addition. Add cocoa, flour and water; beat well. Stir in chopped pecans.

3. Beat egg whites, cream of tartar and salt in small bowl with clean set of beaters until stiff peaks form; carefully fold into chocolate mixture with 1 cup chocolate chips, reserving remaining chips for glaze. Pour mixture into prepared pan.

4. Bake 45 minutes or until top begins to crack slightly. (Cake will not test done in center.) Cool 1 hour. Cover; refrigerate until firm. Loosen cake from side of pan; remove side of pan. Prepare Royal Chip Glaze; pour over cake, allowing to run down sides. With metal spatula, spread glaze evenly on top and sides. Garnish with sweetened whipped cream or pecan halves, if desired. Cover; refrigerate leftover dessert.

ROYAL CHIP GLAZE: Combine remaining 1 cup chocolate chips, and ¼ cup milk in small saucepan. Cook over very low heat, stirring constantly, until chocolate is melted and mixture is smooth; do not boil. Remove from heat; cool, stirring occasionally, until mixture thickens, about 10 to 15 minutes.

3 egg whites, at room temperature

⅛ teaspoon cream of tartar

¾ cup sugar

1 teaspoon vanilla extract

2 tablespoons HERSHEY'S Cocoa

2 cups (12-ounce package) HERSHEY'S Semi-Sweet Chocolate Chips

CHOCOLATE CLOUDS

Makes 2½ dozen cookies

1. Heat oven to 300°F. Cover cookie sheet with parchment paper or foil.

2. Beat egg whites and cream of tartar in large bowl at high speed of mixer until soft peaks form. Gradually add sugar and vanilla, beating well after each addition until stiff peaks hold, sugar is dissolved and mixture is glossy. Sift cocoa onto egg white mixture; gently fold just until combined. Fold in chocolate chips. Drop by heaping tablespoons onto prepared cookie sheet.

3. Bake 35 to 45 minutes or just until dry. Cool slightly; peel paper from cookies. Store, covered, at room temperature.

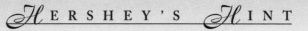

HERSHEY'S HINT

Probably the most popular and often-used extract is vanilla. It is derived from the long, thin pod of a tropical orchid. Vanilla beans are grown in Madagascar, Mexico and Tahiti. Madagascar provides the majority of the world's supply.

Chocolate Clouds

1 can (8 ounces) refrigerated
   quick crescent dinner rolls
2 tablespoons butter or
   margarine, softened
1 tablespoon granulated sugar
2 teaspoons HERSHEY'S
   Cocoa
¼ cup chopped nuts
   Powdered sugar

COCOA NUT BUNDLES

Makes 8 rolls

1. Heat oven to 375°F. On ungreased cookie sheet, unroll dough and separate to form 8 triangles.

2. Combine butter, granulated sugar and cocoa in small bowl. Add nuts; mix thoroughly. Divide chocolate mixture evenly among the triangles, placing on wide ends of triangles. Take dough on either side of mixture and pull up and over mixture, tucking ends under. Continue rolling dough toward the opposite point.

3. Bake 9 to 10 minutes or until golden brown. Sprinkle with powdered sugar; serve warm.

HERSHEY'S HINT

The famous Hershey's Kisses Chocolates were first manufactured on July 1, 1907. In 1990, Hershey's Kisses with almonds were introduced, followed by Hershey's Hugs, with and without almonds, in 1993.

Cocoa Nut Bundles

Almond Custard Sauce
(recipe follows)

3 tablespoons HERSHEY'S
Cocoa

2 tablespoons all-purpose flour

2 tablespoons butter or
margarine, softened

⅓ cup milk

½ teaspoon vanilla extract

⅓ cup sugar, divided
(reserving 1 tablespoon)

2 eggs, separated

CHOCOLATE SOUFFLÉ FOR TWO

Makes 2 servings

1. Prepare Almond Custard Sauce at least 1 hour before serving.

2. Lightly grease and sugar 3-cup soufflé dish. Stir together cocoa and flour in a small bowl. Add butter, blending well.

3. Heat milk in medium saucepan until very hot. Do not boil. Add cocoa mixture; cook over low heat, stirring constantly, until thickened. Remove from heat; stir in vanilla and sugar, reserving 1 tablespoon sugar. Cool slightly. Add egg yolks, one at a time, beating with wooden spoon after each addition; cool to room temperature.

4. Heat oven to 350°F. Beat egg whites in large bowl until soft peaks form; gradually add remaining 1 tablespoon sugar and beat until stiff peaks form. Fold one-fourth of beaten whites into chocolate mixture; carefully fold chocolate mixture into remaining whites. Pour into prepared dish. Bake 25 minutes. Serve soufflé immediately with cool sauce.

ALMOND CUSTARD SAUCE: Heat 1 cup milk in small saucepan over low heat until very hot. Do not boil. Beat 2 egg yolks with 2 tablespoons sugar in small bowl. Return mixture to saucepan; cook over medium-low heat, stirring constantly, until mixture is slightly thickened and coats a metal spoon. Do not boil. Remove from heat; pour into bowl. (If custard should start to curdle, beat vigorously with rotary beater until smooth.) Cool quickly by placing in refrigerator 5 minutes; stir in $1/4$ teaspoon vanilla extract and 1 teaspoon almond-flavored liqueur or $1/4$ teaspoon almond extract. Cover; refrigerate until just before serving.

CHOCOLATE TAPIOCA

Makes 4 to 6 servings

¾ cup sugar

¼ cup HERSHEY'S Cocoa

3 tablespoons quick-cooking tapioca

⅛ teaspoon salt

2¾ cups milk

1 egg, slightly beaten

1 teaspoon vanilla extract

Combine sugar, cocoa, tapioca and salt in medium saucepan; blend in milk and egg. Let stand 5 minutes. Cook over medium heat, stirring constantly, until mixture boils. Remove from heat; stir in vanilla. Pour into bowl; press plastic wrap directly onto surface. Cool; refrigerate. Spoon into individual dessert dishes.

1 can (14 ounces) sweetened
  condensed milk
  (not evaporated milk)

⅓ cup HERSHEY'S Cocoa

3 tablespoons butter or
  margarine

2 teaspoons powdered instant
  coffee or espresso,
  dissolved in 2 teaspoons
  hot water

2 cups (1 pint) cold whipping
  cream

COCOA CAPPUCCINO MOUSSE

Makes 8 servings

1. Combine sweetened condensed milk, cocoa, butter and coffee in medium saucepan. Cook over low heat, stirring constantly, until butter melts and mixture is smooth. Remove from heat; cool.

2. Beat whipping cream in large bowl until stiff. Gradually fold chocolate mixture into whipped cream. Spoon into dessert dishes. Refrigerate until set, about 2 hours. Garnish as desired.

Prep Time: 15 minutes
Cook Time: 10 minutes
Chill Time: 2 hours

HERSHEY'S HINT

Mousse is a French word meaning froth or foam. It can be sweet or savory, but is always light and airy due to the addition of beaten egg whites and/or cream. When most people think of mousse, they think of chocolate.

Cocoa Cappuccino Mousse

1 ripe medium banana

1½ cups orange juice

1 cup (½ pint) half-and-half

½ cup sugar

¼ cup HERSHEY'S Cocoa

REFRESHING COCOA-FRUIT SHERBET

Makes 8 servings

1. Slice banana into blender container. Add orange juice; cover and blend until smooth. Add remaining ingredients; cover and blend well. Pour into 8- or 9-inch square pan. Cover; freeze until hard around edges.

2. Spoon partially frozen mixture into blender container. Cover; blend until smooth but not melted. Pour into 1-quart mold. Cover; freeze until firm. Unmold onto cold plate and slice. Garnish as desired.

VARIATION: Add 2 teaspoons orange-flavored liqueur with orange juice.

HERSHEY'S HINT

Bananas are high in fiber and great flavor, but low in calories. Naturally sweet bananas are a good source of vitamin B6, and also contain a wide assortment of other nutrients, including vitamin C and potassium.

Refreshing Cocoa-Fruit Sherbet

Chocolate Crumb Crust
(recipe follows)

1 package (3 ounces) cream
cheese, softened

½ cup sugar

½ cup HERSHEY'S Cocoa

¼ cup milk

5 cups frozen non-dairy
whipped topping, thawed
(about 12 ounces), divided

¼ to ½ teaspoon peppermint
extract

Green food color

Mint leaves (optional)

LUCK OF THE IRISH DESSERT SQUARES

Makes 6 to 9 servings

1. Prepare Chocolate Crumb Crust.

2. Beat cream cheese in medium bowl until fluffy. Gradually add sugar, beating until well blended. Add cocoa alternately with milk, beating until smooth. Gradually fold in 3 cups whipped topping; spoon mixture over crumb crust.

3. Stir together remaining 2 cups whipped topping, peppermint extract and a few drops of food color in small bowl; spread over chocolate layer. Cover; refrigerate about 6 hours or until set. Cut into squares. Garnish with mint leaves, if desired. Cover; refrigerate leftover dessert.

CHOCOLATE CRUMB CRUST: Combine 1 cup graham cracker crumbs, $1/4$ cup sugar, $1/4$ cup HERSHEY'S Cocoa and 5 tablespoons melted butter or margarine in small bowl; stir until well blended. Press mixture onto bottom of 9-inch square pan. Makes 1 (9-inch) crust.

1½ **cups (12-ounce can) evaporated skim milk, divided**

⅓ **cup sugar**

¼ **cup HERSHEY'S Cocoa**

1 **envelope unflavored gelatin**

¾ **teaspoon powdered instant coffee**

1 **teaspoon vanilla extract**

MOCHA MOUSSE

Makes 8 servings

1. Pour $^3/_4$ cup evaporated milk into large bowl; place in freezer until milk begins to freeze around edges.

2. Stir together sugar, cocoa, gelatin and instant coffee in small saucepan. Stir in remaining $^3/_4$ cup evaporated milk. Let stand 2 minutes. Cook over medium heat, stirring constantly, until mixture is smooth and gelatin has completely dissolved. Pour into medium bowl; stir in vanilla. Cool to room temperature, stirring occasionally.

3. Beat cold evaporated milk on high speed of mixer until soft peaks form. Add cocoa mixture, stirring gently until well blended. Pour into individual dessert dishes. Refrigerate about 1 hour before serving.

187

HERSHEY'S HINT

Extracts are very concentrated flavorings derived from a variety of foods. Well-known extracts include vanilla, lemon and almond. A pure extract is made by distilling and concentrating a food's natural oils and mixing them with alcohol. Small amounts, usually a teaspoon or less, provide a lot of flavor impact without adding volume or moisture.

1½ cups (3 sticks) plus
6 tablespoons butter
or margarine, divided

2 cups granulated sugar

2 teaspoons vanilla extract

4 eggs

¾ cup HERSHEY'S Cocoa

1 cup all-purpose flour

½ teaspoon baking powder

2⅔ cups powdered sugar

1 tablespoon plus 1 teaspoon
water

1 teaspoon mint extract

4 drops green food color

1 cup HERSHEY'S Semi-Sweet
Chocolate Chips

IRISH CHOCOLATE MINT DESSERT

Makes 24 servings

1. Heat oven to 350°F. Grease 13×9×2-inch baking pan.

2. Place 1 cup (2 sticks) butter in large microwave-safe bowl; cover. Microwave at HIGH (100%) 2 minutes or until melted. Stir in granulated sugar and vanilla. Add eggs; beat well. Add cocoa, flour and baking powder; beat until well blended. Pour batter into prepared pan.

3. Bake 30 to 35 minutes or until wooden pick inserted in center comes out clean. Cool completely in pan on wire rack.

4. Prepare mint cream center by combining powdered sugar, ½ cup (1 stick) butter, water, mint extract and food color. Beat until smooth. Spread evenly on brownie. Cover; refrigerate until cold.

5. Prepare chocolate glaze by placing remaining 6 tablespoons butter and chocolate chips in small microwave-safe bowl. Microwave at HIGH (100%) 1 minute or until mixture is smooth when stirred. Cool slightly; pour over chilled dessert. Cover; refrigerate at least 1 hour before serving. Cover; refrigerate leftover dessert.

Irish Chocolate Mint Dessert

⅔ cup sugar

3 tablespoons HERSHEY'S Cocoa

1¾ cups water

3 tablespoons frozen pineapple juice concentrate, thawed

1 tablespoon golden rum or ½ teaspoon rum extract

CARIBBEAN FREEZE

Makes 6 servings (¾ cup each)

1. Stir together sugar and cocoa in medium saucepan; stir in water. Cook over medium heat, stirring occasionally, until mixture comes to a boil. Reduce heat; simmer 3 minutes, stirring occasionally. Cool completely.

2. Stir concentrate and rum into chocolate mixture. Cover; refrigerate until cold, about 6 hours.

3. Pour cold mixture into 1-quart container of ice cream freezer. Freeze according to manufacturer's directions. Garnish as desired.

HERSHEY'S HINT

Have fun with this delicious frozen dessert and garnish it with pineapple slices, maraschino cherries or fresh kiwi slices. For a real island twist, serve this treat in hollowed coconuts.

Caribbean Freeze

¾ cup HERSHEY'S Cocoa

1 cup sugar, divided

½ cup all-purpose flour

¼ teaspoon salt

2 cups milk

6 egg yolks, well beaten

2 tablespoons butter or margarine

1 teaspoon vanilla extract

8 egg whites

¼ teaspoon cream of tartar

Sweetened whipped cream

HOT CHOCOLATE SOUFFLÉ

Makes 8 to 10 servings

1. Adjust oven rack to lowest position. Heat oven to 350°F. Lightly butter $2^{1}/_{2}$-quart soufflé dish; sprinkle with sugar. For collar, cut a length of heavy-duty aluminum foil to fit around soufflé dish; fold in thirds lengthwise. Lightly butter one side. Attach foil, buttered side in, around outside of dish, allowing foil to extend at least 2 inches above dish. Secure foil with tape or string.

2. Stir together cocoa, $^{3}/_{4}$ cup sugar, flour and salt in large saucepan; gradually stir in milk. Cook over medium heat, stirring constantly with wire whisk, until mixture boils; remove from heat. Gradually stir small amount of chocolate mixture into beaten egg yolks; blend well. Add egg mixture to chocolate mixture in pan, blending well. Cook and stir 1 minute. Add butter and vanilla, stirring until blended. Set aside; cool 20 minutes.

3. Beat egg whites with cream of tartar in large bowl until soft peaks form; gradually add remaining $^{1}/_{4}$ cup sugar, beating until stiff peaks form. Gently fold about one-third of beaten egg white mixture into chocolate mixture. Lightly fold chocolate mixture, half at a time, into remaining beaten egg white mixture just until blended; do not overfold.

continued on page 194

Hot Chocolate Soufflé

Hot Chocolate Soufflé, continued

4. Gently pour mixture into prepared dish; smooth top with spatula. Gently place dish in larger baking pan; pour hot water into larger pan to depth of 1 inch.

5. Bake 65 to 70 minutes or until puffed and set. Remove soufflé dish from water. Carefully remove foil. Serve immediately with sweetened whipped cream.

CHOCOLATE-AMARETTO ICE

Makes 4 servings

¾ cup sugar

½ cup HERSHEY'S Cocoa

2 cups (1 pint) light cream or half-and-half

2 tablespoons Amaretto (almond flavored liqueur)

Sliced almonds (optional)

1. Stir together sugar and cocoa in small saucepan; gradually stir in light cream. Cook over low heat, stirring constantly, until sugar dissolves and mixture is smooth and hot. Do not boil.

2. Remove from heat; stir in liqueur. Pour into 8-inch square pan. Cover; freeze until firm, stirring several times before mixture freezes. Scoop into dessert dishes. Serve frozen. Garnish with sliced almonds, if desired.

½ cup (1 stick) butter or margarine, softened

1 ¼ cups granulated sugar

1 teaspoon vanilla extract

4 eggs

⅔ cup milk

½ teaspoon powdered instant coffee

⅔ cup all-purpose flour

⅔ cup HERSHEY'S Cocoa

1 ½ teaspoons baking powder

1 cup (½ pint) cold whipping cream

2 tablespoons powdered sugar

INDIVIDUAL FUDGE SOUFFLÉS

Makes 8 servings

1. Heat oven to 325°F. Grease and sugar eight 6-ounce ramekins or custard cups; set aside.

2. Beat butter, granulated sugar and vanilla in large bowl until fluffy. Add eggs, one at a time, beating well after each addition. Scald milk; remove from heat and add powdered coffee, stirring until dissolved. Combine flour, cocoa and baking powder; add alternately with milk mixture to butter mixture. Beat 1 minute on medium speed of mixer. Divide batter evenly among prepared ramekins. Place ramekins in two 8-inch square pans; place pans in oven. Pour hot water into pans to a depth of $1/8$ inch.

3. Bake 45 to 50 minutes, adding more water if necessary or until wooden pick inserted in centers comes out clean. Remove pans from oven; allow ramekins to stand in water 5 minutes. Remove ramekins from water; cool slightly. Serve in ramekins or invert onto dessert dishes. Beat cream with powdered sugar until stiff; spoon onto warm soufflés.

1 package (6-serving size, 4.6 ounces) vanilla cook & serve pudding and pie filling mix*

3½ cups milk

1 cup REESE'S Peanut Butter Chips

1 cup HERSHEY'S Semi-Sweet *or* Milk Chocolate MINI KISSES Baking Pieces

Whipped topping (optional)

Additional MINI KISSES or grated chocolate

Do not use instant pudding mix.

TWO GREAT TASTES PUDDING PARFAITS

Makes 4 to 6 servings

1. Combine pudding mix and 3½ cups milk in large heavy saucepan (rather than amount listed in package directions). Cook over medium heat, stirring constantly, until mixture comes to a full boil. Remove from heat; divide hot mixture between 2 heat-proof medium bowls.

2. Immediately stir peanut butter chips into mixture in one bowl and Mini Kisses into second bowl. Stir both mixtures until chips are melted and mixture is smooth. Cool slightly, stirring occasionally.

3. Alternately layer peanut butter and chocolate mixtures in parfait dishes, wine glasses or dessert dishes. Place plastic wrap directly onto surface of each dessert; refrigerate about 6 hours. Garnish with whipped topping, if desired, and Mini Kisses.

Two Great Tastes Pudding Parfaits

2 packages (3 ounces each)
  ladyfingers, split

1 package (10 ounces) frozen
  strawberries in syrup,
  thawed and drained

2 envelopes unflavored gelatin

2 cups milk, divided

1 cup sugar

⅓ cup HERSHEY'S Cocoa or
  HERSHEY'S Dutch
  Processed Cocoa

¼ cup (½ stick) butter or
  margarine

1 teaspoon vanilla extract

2 cups frozen non-dairy
  whipped topping, thawed

  Additional whipped topping
  (optional)

  Fresh strawberries (optional)

  Mint leaves (optional)

Easy Chocoberry Cream Dessert

Makes 10 to 12 servings

1. Place ladyfingers, cut sides in, on bottom and around side of 9-inch springform pan.

2. Purée strawberries in food processor. Sprinkle gelatin over 1 cup milk in medium saucepan; let stand 2 minutes to soften. Add sugar, cocoa and butter. Cook over medium heat, stirring constantly, until mixture is hot and gelatin is completely dissolved. Remove from heat; stir in remaining 1 cup milk, vanilla and puréed strawberries. Refrigerate until mixture begins to thicken.

3. Fold 2 cups whipped topping into gelatin mixture. Pour mixture into prepared pan. Cover; refrigerate until mixture is firm. Just before serving, remove side of pan. Garnish with additional whipped topping, fresh strawberries and mint, if desired. Cover; refrigerate leftover dessert.

Easy Chocoberry Cream Dessert

½ cup nonfat milk

½ cup plain nonfat yogurt

⅓ cup sugar

¼ cup orange juice

1 egg, slightly beaten

1 tablespoon freshly grated orange peel

3 cups all-purpose biscuit baking mix

½ cup HERSHEY'S MINI CHIPS Semi-Sweet Chocolate

ORANGE CHOCOLATE CHIP BREAD

Makes 1 loaf (16 slices)

1. Heat oven to 350°F. Grease 9×5×3-inch loaf pan or spray with vegetable cooking spray.

2. Stir together milk, yogurt, sugar, orange juice, egg and orange peel in large bowl; add baking mix. With spoon, beat until well blended, about 1 minute. Stir in Mini Chips. Pour into prepared pan.

3. Bake 45 to 50 minutes or until wooden pick inserted in center comes out clean. Cool 10 minutes; remove from pan to wire rack. Cool completely before slicing. Garnish as desired. Wrap leftover bread in foil or plastic wrap. Store at room temperature or freeze for longer storage.

NUTRIENTS PER SERVING (1 SLICE):

Calories: 160, Protein: 3g, Carbohydrate: 27g, Total Fat: 4g, (Saturated Fat: 1.5g), Cholesterol: 10mg, Sodium: 270mg

Orange Chocolate Chip Bread

1 envelope unflavored gelatin

¼ cup cold water

2 tablespoons reduced-calorie tub margarine

1½ cups cold nonfat milk, divided

½ cup sugar

⅓ cup HERSHEY'S Cocoa *or* HERSHEY'S Dutch Processed Cocoa

2½ teaspoons vanilla extract, divided

1 envelope (1.3 ounces) dry whipped topping mix

LUSCIOUS COLD CHOCOLATE SOUFFLÉS

Makes 6 servings

1. Measure lengths of foil to fit around 6 small soufflé dishes (about 4 ounces each); fold in thirds lengthwise. Tape securely to outsides of dishes to form collars, allowing collars to extend 1 inch above rims of dishes. Lightly grease insides of foil.*

2. Sprinkle gelatin over water in small microwave-safe bowl; let stand 2 minutes to soften. Microwave at HIGH (100%) 40 seconds; stir thoroughly. Stir in margarine until melted; let stand 2 minutes or until gelatin is completely dissolved.

3. Stir together 1 cup milk, sugar, cocoa and 2 teaspoons vanilla in small bowl. Beat on low speed of mixer while gradually pouring in gelatin mixture. Beat until well blended.

4. Prepare topping mix as directed on package, using remaining ¹/₂ cup milk and remaining ¹/₂ teaspoon vanilla; carefully fold into chocolate mixture until well blended. Spoon into prepared soufflé dishes, filling ¹/₂ inch from tops of collars. Cover; refrigerate until firm, about 3 hours. Carefully remove foil. Garnish as desired.

Six (6-ounce) custard cups may be used in place of soufflé dishes; omit foil collars.

NUTRIENTS PER SERVING:

Calories: 160, Protein: 4g, Carbohydrate: 27g, Total Fat: 3.5g, (Saturated Fat: 2g), Cholesterol: 0mg, Sodium: 85mg

Luscious Cold Chocolate Soufflés

2 containers (8 ounces each)
   lowfat vanilla yogurt, no
   gelatin added

2 cups (1 pint) fresh
   strawberries, rinsed and
   drained

¼ cup sugar

¼ cup HERSHEY'S Cocoa *or*
   HERSHEY'S Dutch
   Processed Cocoa

2 tablespoons hot water

2 teaspoons vanilla extract,
   divided

½ to 1 teaspoon freshly grated
   orange peel (optional)

2 envelopes (1.3 ounces each)
   dry whipped topping mix

1 cup cold nonfat milk

2 large bananas, sliced

FRUIT IN A CHOCOLATE CLOUD

Makes 12 servings (¹/₃ cup each)

1. Prepare Yogurt Cheese about 24 hours before needed. Line non-rusting colander or sieve with large piece of double thickness cheesecloth or large coffee filter; place colander over deep bowl. Spoon yogurt into prepared colander; cover with plastic wrap. Refrigerate until liquid no longer drains from yogurt, about 24 hours. Remove yogurt cheese from cheesecloth; discard liquid.

2. Reserve 3 strawberries for garnish; set aside. Remove hulls of remaining strawberries; cut strawberries in half vertically; set aside.

3. Stir together sugar, cocoa and water in small bowl until smooth and well blended. Stir in 1 teaspoon vanilla. Gradually stir in Yogurt Cheese and orange peel, if desired; blend thoroughly.

4. Prepare topping mix in large bowl as directed on package, using 1 cup milk and remaining 1 teaspoon vanilla; fold into chocolate mixture. *continued on page 206*

Fruit in a Chocolate Cloud

Fruit in a Chocolate Cloud, continued

5. Carefully spoon half of chocolate mixture into 1^1/$_2$-quart glass serving dish; place one-half of strawberry halves, cut sides out, around inside of entire bowl. Layer banana slices over chocolate mixture. Cut remaining strawberry halves into smaller pieces; layer over banana slices. Carefully spread remaining chocolate mixture over fruit. Cover; refrigerate several hours before serving. Garnish with reserved strawberries. Cover; refrigerate leftover dessert.

NUTRIENTS PER SERVING:

Calories: 120, Protein: 4g, Carbohydrate: 22g, Total Fat: 2g, (Saturated Fat: 0g), Cholesterol: 0mg, Sodium: 35mg

1 envelope (1.3 ounces) dry whipped topping mix

½ cup cold lowfat 2% milk

1 teaspoon vanilla extract

¼ cup sugar

¼ cup HERSHEY'S Cocoa or HERSHEY'S Dutch Processed Cocoa

10 tablespoons chopped peaches

5 tablespoons (about 10 wafers) vanilla wafer crumbs

Peach slices (optional)

PEACHY CHOCOLATE MOUSSE PARFAITS

Makes 5 servings

Combine whipped topping mix, milk and vanilla in small bowl; beat until stiff. Stir together sugar and cocoa; gradually add to whipped topping, beating until smooth. Spoon mousse into ^{1}/$_3$ cup measure; place half of this amount into bottom of parfait or wine glass. Layer 2 tablespoons chopped peaches, then 1 tablespoon vanilla wafer crumbs over mousse. Top with remaining mousse. Repeat procedure for remaining 4 glasses. Cover; refrigerate until serving time. Garnish with peach slice, if desired.

NUTRIENTS PER SERVING:

Calories: 190, Protein: 4g, Carbohydrate: 31g, Total Fat: 5g, (Saturated Fat: 3g), Cholesterol: 5mg, Sodium: 45mg

1 ¼ cups all-purpose flour

1 cup sugar

1 cup nonfat milk

⅓ cup HERSHEY'S Cocoa
  or HERSHEY'S Dutch
  Processed Cocoa

⅓ cup unsweetened
  applesauce

1 tablespoon white vinegar

1 teaspoon baking soda

½ teaspoon vanilla extract

Toppings (optional): Frozen
  light non-dairy whipped
  topping, thawed; REESE'S
  Peanut Butter Chips,
  sliced; strawberries;
  chopped almonds;
  raspberries

FOUR WAY FUDGEY CHOCOLATE CAKE

Makes 12 servings

1. Heat oven to 350°F. Spray 9-inch square baking pan or 11×7×2-inch baking pan with vegetable cooking spray.

2. Stir together flour, sugar, milk, cocoa, applesauce, vinegar, baking soda and vanilla in large bowl; beat on low speed of mixer until blended. Pour batter into prepared pan.

3. Bake 30 to 35 minutes or until wooden pick inserted in center comes out clean. Cool completely in pan on wire rack.

4. Spoon whipped topping into pastry bag fitted with star tip; pipe stars in two lines to divide cake into four squares or rectangles. Using plain tip, pipe lattice design into one square; place peanut butter chips on lattice. Place strawberries into another square. Sprinkle almonds into third square. Place raspberries into remaining square.

5. Serve immediately. Cover; refrigerate leftover cake. Store ungarnished cake, covered, at room temperature.

NUTRIENTS PER SERVING (NO GARNISHES):

Calories: 170, Protein: 4g, Carbohydrate: 35g, Total Fat: 2g, (Saturated Fat: 1g), Cholesterol: 0mg, Sodium: 120mg

2 cups (1 pound) nonfat cottage cheese

¾ cup liquid egg substitute

⅔ cup sugar

4 ounces (½ of 8-ounce package) Neufchâtel cheese (⅓ less fat cream cheese), softened

⅓ cup HERSHEY'S Cocoa *or* HERSHEY'S Dutch Processed Cocoa

½ teaspoon vanilla extract

Yogurt Topping (recipe follows)

Sliced strawberries or mandarin orange segments (optional)

LUSCIOUS CHOCOLATE CHEESECAKE

Makes 9 servings

1. Heat oven to 300°F. Spray 9-inch springform pan with vegetable cooking spray.

2. Place cottage cheese, egg substitute, sugar, Neufchâtel cheese, cocoa and vanilla in food processor; process until smooth. Pour into prepared pan.

3. Bake 35 minutes or until edges are set.

4. Meanwhile, prepare Yogurt Topping. Carefully spread topping over cheesecake. Continue baking 5 minutes. Remove from oven to wire rack. With knife, loosen cheesecake from side of pan. Cool completely.

5. Cover; refrigerate until chilled. Remove side of pan. Serve with strawberries or mandarin orange segments, if desired. Refrigerate leftover cheesecake.

YOGURT TOPPING

⅔ cup plain nonfat yogurt

2 tablespoons sugar

Stir together yogurt and sugar in small bowl until well blended.

NUTRIENTS PER SERVING:

Calories: 210, Protein: 14g, Carbohydrate: 26g, Total Fat: 6g, (Saturated Fat: 2.5g), Cholesterol: 15mg, Sodium: 270mg

Luscious Chocolate Cheesecake

⅓ cup HERSHEY'S Cocoa

1 package (about 15 ounces) "two-step" angel food cake mix

2 envelopes (1.3 ounces each) dry whipped topping mix

1 cup cold nonfat milk

1 teaspoon vanilla extract

1 cup strawberry purée*

Strawberries

*Mash 2 cups sliced fresh strawberries (or frozen berries, thawed) in blender or food processor. Cover; blend until smooth. Purée should measure 1 cup.

ELEGANT CHOCOLATE ANGEL TORTE

Makes about 16 servings

1. Move oven rack to lowest position.

2. Sift cocoa over contents of cake flour packet; stir to blend. Proceed with mixing cake as directed on package. Bake and cool as directed for 10-inch tube pan. Carefully run knife along side of pan to loosen cake; remove from pan. Using serrated knife, slice cake horizontally into four layers.

3. Prepare whipped topping mix as directed on package, using 1 cup milk and 1 teaspoon vanilla. Blend in strawberry purée.

4. Place bottom cake layer on serving plate; spread with ¼ of topping. Set next cake layer on top; spread with ¼ of topping. Continue layering cake and topping. Garnish with strawberries. Refrigerate until ready to serve. Slice cake with sharp serrated knife, cutting with gentle sawing motion. Cover; refrigerate leftover cake.

Prep Time: 30 minutes
Bake Time: 45 minutes
Cool Time: 2 hours

NUTRIENTS PER SERVING (1 PIECE):

Calories: 150, Protein: 4g, Carbohydrate: 28g, Total Fat: 2g, (Saturated Fat: 2g), Cholesterol: 0mg, Sodium: 210mg

Elegant Chocolate Angel Torte

2 egg whites

¼ teaspoon cream of tartar

Dash salt

¾ cup sugar

¼ teaspoon vanilla extract

Chocolate Filling (page 214)

1 package (10 ounces) frozen strawberries in syrup, thawed

CHOCOLATE-FILLED MERINGUE SHELLS WITH STRAWBERRY SAUCE

Makes 10 servings

1. Heat oven to 275°F. Line 10 muffin cups (2½ inches in diameter) with paper bake cups.

2. Beat egg whites with cream of tartar and salt in small bowl at high speed of mixer until soft peaks form. Beat in sugar, 1 tablespoon at a time, beating well after each addition until stiff peaks hold their shape, sugar is dissolved and mixture is glossy. Fold in vanilla.

3. Spoon about 3 tablespoons mixture in each muffin cup. Using back of spoon or small spatula, push mixture up sides of muffin cups to form a well in center.

4. Bake 1 hour or until meringues turn delicate cream color and feel dry to the touch. Cool in pan on wire rack.

5. Before serving, carefully remove paper from shells. Prepare Chocolate Filling; for each serving, spoon 1 heaping tablespoon into meringue shell.

6. Place strawberries with syrup in blender container. Cover; blend until smooth. Spoon over filled shells. Garnish as desired. To store leftover unfilled shells, peel paper bake cups from shells; store shells loosely covered at room temperature.

continued on page 214

Chocolate-Filled Meringue Shells with Strawberry Sauce

Chocolate-Filled Meringue Shells with Strawberry Sauce, continued

CHOCOLATE FILLING: Beat 4 ounces ($^1/_2$ of 8-ounce package) softened Neufchâtel cheese ($^1/_3$ less fat cream cheese) and $^1/_4$ cup HERSHEY'S Cocoa in small bowl on medium speed of mixer until blended. Gradually add $^3/_4$ cup powdered sugar, beating until well blended. Fold in 1 cup frozen light non-dairy whipped topping, thawed.

NUTRIENTS PER SERVING:

Calories: 170, Protein: 4g, Carbohydrate: 28g, Total Fat: 5g, (Saturated Fat: 3.5g), Cholesterol: 10mg, Sodium: 180mg

⅓ **cup sugar**

¼ **cup cornstarch**

3 **tablespoons HERSHEY'S Cocoa *or* HERSHEY'S Dutch Processed Cocoa**

2 **cups nonfat milk**

1 **teaspoon vanilla extract**

1 **packaged graham cracker crumb crust (6 ounces)**

Frozen light non-dairy whipped topping, thawed (optional)

Assorted fresh fruit (optional)

CHOCOLATE CREAM PIE WITH NONFAT MILK

Makes 10 servings

1. Stir together sugar, cornstarch and cocoa in large microwave-safe bowl; gradually stir in milk. Microwave at HIGH (100%) 2 minutes; stir well. Microwave at HIGH 2 to 5 minutes or until mixture just begins to boil; stir well. Microwave at HIGH 30 seconds to 1 minute or until mixture is very hot and thickened. Add vanilla. Pour into crust.

2. Press plastic wrap directly onto surface; refrigerate several hours or until set. Garnish with whipped topping and fruit, if desired. Store, covered, in refrigerator.

NUTRIENTS PER SERVING:

Calories: 160, Protein: 3g, Carbohydrate: 26g, Total Fat: 5g, (Saturated Fat: 1g), Cholesterol: 0mg, Sodium: 150mg

2 envelopes unflavored gelatin

½ cup cold water

1 cup boiling water

1 ⅓ cups nonfat dry milk powder

⅓ cup HERSHEY'S Cocoa *or*
    HERSHEY'S Dutch
    Processed Cocoa

1 tablespoon vanilla extract

    Dash salt

    Granulated sugar substitute
    to equal 14 teaspoons
    sugar

8 large ice cubes

LIGHTER THAN AIR CHOCOLATE DELIGHT

Makes 8 servings

1. Sprinkle gelatin over cold water in blender container; let stand 4 minutes to soften. Gently stir with rubber spatula, scraping gelatin particles off sides; add boiling water to gelatin mixture. Cover; blend until gelatin dissolves. Add milk powder, cocoa, vanilla and salt; blend on medium speed until well mixed. Add sugar substitute and ice cubes; blend on high speed until ice is crushed and mixture is smooth and fluffy.

2. Immediately pour into 4-cup mold. Cover; refrigerate until firm. Unmold onto serving plate.

NOTE: Eight individual dessert dishes may be used in place of 4-cup mold, if desired.

NUTRIENTS PER SERVING:

Calories: 60, Protein: 6g, Carbohydrate: 9g, Total Fat: 0g, (Saturated Fat: 0g), Cholesterol: 0mg, Sodium: 210mg

1 envelope unflavored gelatin

1¾ cups cold water

⅔ cup nonfat dry milk powder

2 egg yolks, slightly beaten

3 tablespoons HERSHEY'S Cocoa

¼ teaspoon salt

½ cup sugar or equivalent amount of granulated sugar substitute

2 teaspoons vanilla extract

½ cup frozen light non-dairy whipped topping, thawed

Assorted fresh fruit, cut up (optional)

Additional frozen light non-dairy whipped topping, thawed (optional)

Additional HERSHEY'S Cocoa (optional)

WAIST-WATCHER'S COCOA DESSERT

Makes 6 servings

1. Sprinkle gelatin over water in medium saucepan; let stand 5 minutes to soften. Add milk powder, egg yolks, 3 tablespoons cocoa and salt. Cook over medium heat, stirring constantly, until mixture begins to boil; remove from heat. Stir in sugar and vanilla. Pour mixture into large bowl. Refrigerate, stirring occasionally, until mixture mounds slightly when dropped from spoon, about 1 hour.

2. Fold ½ cup whipped topping into chocolate mixture. Pour into 6 individual dessert dishes. Cover; refrigerate until firm, about 4 hours. Garnish individual dessert dishes with assorted fresh fruit or additional whipped topping, sprinkled with additional cocoa, if desired.

NOTE: A 3-cup mold may be used in place of individual dessert dishes, if desired.

NUTRIENTS PER SERVING:

Calories: 160, Protein: 7g, Carbohydrate: 26g, Total Fat: 3g, (Saturated Fat: 1.5g), Cholesterol: 70mg, Sodium: 150mg

Waist-Watcher's Cocoa Dessert

¼ cup (½ stick) corn oil spread (60% oil)

½ cup sugar

1 egg white

1¼ cups all-purpose flour

¼ cup HERSHEY'S Cocoa *or* HERSHEY'S Dutch Processed Cocoa

¾ teaspoon cream of tartar

½ teaspoon baking soda

Dash salt

½ cup strawberry all-fruit spread

White Chip Drizzle (recipe follows)

CHOCO-LOWFAT STRAWBERRY SHORTBREAD BARS

Makes 3 dozen bars

1. Heat oven to 375°F. Lightly spray 13×9×2-inch baking pan with vegetable cooking spray. Combine corn oil spread and sugar in medium bowl; beat on medium speed of mixer until well blended. Add egg white; beat until well blended. Stir together flour, cocoa, cream of tartar, baking soda and salt; gradually add to sugar mixture, beating well. Gently press mixture onto bottom of prepared pan.

2. Bake 10 to 12 minutes or just until set. Cool completely in pan on wire rack. Spread fruit spread evenly over crust. Cut into bars or other desired shapes with cookie cutters. Prepare White Chip Drizzle; drizzle over tops of bars. Let stand until set.

WHITE CHIP DRIZZLE

⅓ cup HERSHEY'S Premier White Chips

½ teaspoon shortening (do not use butter, margarine, spread or oil)

Place white chips and shortening in small microwave-safe bowl. Microwave at HIGH (100% power) 30 seconds; stir. If necessary, microwave at HIGH an additional 15 seconds at a time, stirring after each heating, just until chips are melted when stirred. Use immediately.

NUTRIENTS PER SERVING (1 BAR):

Calories: 60, Protein: 1g, Carbohydrate: 10g, Total Fat: 1.5g, (Saturated Fat: 0.5g), Cholesterol: 0mg, Sodium: 70mg

Choco-Lowfat Strawberry Shortbread Bars

¾ cup water

½ cup (1 stick) 60% vegetable oil spread, melted

2 egg whites, slightly beaten

1 teaspoon vanilla extract

2¼ cups HERSHEY'S Basic Cocoa Baking Mix (recipe follows)

2 teaspoons powdered sugar

2 teaspoons HERSHEY'S Cocoa (optional)

FUDGEY CHOCOLATE CUPCAKES

Makes 16 cupcakes

1. Heat oven to 350°F. Line 16 muffin cups (2½ inches in diameter) with foil or paper bake cups.

2. Stir together water, melted spread, egg whites and vanilla in large bowl. Prepare Basic Cocoa Baking Mix; add to egg white mixture. Beat on low speed of mixer until blended. Fill muffin cups ²/₃ full with batter.

3. Bake 20 to 25 minutes or until wooden pick inserted in centers comes out clean. Remove from pans to wire racks. Cool completely. Sift powdered sugar over tops of cupcakes. If desired, partially cover part of each cupcake with paper cutout. Sift cocoa over exposed powdered sugar. Carefully lift off cutout. Store, covered, at room temperature.

HERSHEY'S BASIC COCOA BAKING MIX: Stir together 4½ cups all-purpose flour, 2¾ cups sugar, 1¼ cups HERSHEY'S Cocoa, 1 tablespoon plus ½ teaspoon baking powder, 1¾ teaspoons salt and 1¼ teaspoons baking soda. Store in airtight container in cool, dry place for up to 1 month. Stir before using. Makes 8 cups mix.

NUTRIENTS PER SERVING (1 CUPCAKE):

Calories: 70, Protein: 1g, Carbohydrate: 3g, Total Fat: 6g, (Saturated Fat: 2g), Cholesterol: 5mg, Sodium: 85mg

Fudgey Chocolate Cupcakes

6 tablespoons corn oil spread
   (56 to 60% oil)
1 cup sugar
½ cup HERSHEY'S Cocoa
1 teaspoon vanilla extract
2 egg whites, slightly beaten
½ cup all-purpose flour
¼ cup finely chopped walnuts
   Easy Drizzle (recipe follows)

HERSHEY'S LIGHT DRIZZLED BROWNIES

Makes 21 brownies

1. Heat oven to 350°F. Lightly spray 8-inch square baking pan with vegetable cooking spray.

2. Melt corn oil spread in medium saucepan over low heat. Add sugar; stir until well blended. Remove from heat; stir in cocoa and vanilla. Add egg whites; stir to blend. Stir in flour and walnuts. Spread batter into prepared pan.

3. Bake 25 minutes or until edges begin to pull away from sides of pan. Cool in pan on wire rack. Prepare Easy Drizzle; drizzle over top of brownies. Cut into bars.

EASY DRIZZLE: Stir together $1/3$ cup powdered sugar, $1^1/_2$ teaspoons lowfat 2% milk, 1 or 2 drops green food color and few drops mint extract, if desired, in small bowl until of drizzling consistency.

NUTRIENTS PER SERVING (1 BROWNIE):

Calories: 110, Protein: 3g, Carbohydrate: 17g, Total Fat: 3.5g, (Saturated Fat: 1g), Cholesterol: 0mg, Sodium: 40mg

½ cup all-purpose flour

¼ cup HERSHEY'S Dutch Processed Cocoa *or* HERSHEY'S Cocoa

1 teaspoon baking powder

4 eggs

⅓ cup sugar

1 teaspoon vanilla extract

2 cups (1 pint) vanilla nonfat frozen yogurt, slightly softened

Powdered sugar (optional)

TRIMTIME CHOCOLATE CAKE ROLL

Makes 12 servings

1. Heat oven to 400°F. Spray 15½×10½×1-inch jelly-roll pan with vegetable cooking spray. Line with wax paper; spray again.

2. Sift together flour, cocoa and baking powder. Beat eggs, sugar and vanilla in small bowl until pale in color, about 5 minutes. Fold in cocoa mixture; spread batter into prepared pan.

3. Bake 5 to 7 minutes or until top springs back when touched lightly in center. Invert cake onto clean towel; remove wax paper. Roll up cake with towel from short side. Cool completely on wire rack.

4. Unroll cake; spread with frozen yogurt. Reroll cake without towel; press seam side down. Cover; freeze until firm. Sprinkle top lightly with powdered sugar, if desired. Cover; freeze leftover cake roll.

NUTRIENTS PER SERVING:

Calories: 70, Protein: 4g, Carbohydrate: 11g, Total Fat: 1.5g, (Saturated Fat: 0.5g), Cholesterol: 65mg, Sodium: 60mg

1 envelope unflavored gelatin

½ cup cold water

¾ cup sugar

½ cup HERSHEY'S Cocoa

1 ¼ cups evaporated nonfat milk

1 teaspoon vanilla extract

2 cups frozen light non-dairy
    whipped topping, thawed,
    divided

⅛ teaspoon mint extract

6 to 7 drops green food color

SHAMROCK PARFAITS

Makes 8 servings

1. Sprinkle gelatin over water in medium saucepan; let stand 2 minutes to soften. Cook over low heat, stirring constantly, until gelatin is completely dissolved, about 3 minutes. In small bowl, stir together sugar and cocoa; add gradually to gelatin mixture, stirring with whisk until well blended. Continue to cook over low heat, stirring constantly, until sugar is dissolved, about 3 minutes. Remove from heat. Stir in evaporated milk and vanilla. Pour mixture into large bowl. Refrigerate, stirring occasionally, until mixture mounds slightly when dropped from spoon, about 20 minutes.

2. Fold ¹/₂ cup whipped topping into chocolate mixture. Divide about half of mixture evenly among 8 parfait or wine glasses. Stir extract and food color into remaining 1¹/₂ cups topping; divide evenly among glasses. Spoon remaining chocolate mixture over topping in each glass. Garnish as desired. Serve immediately or cover and refrigerate until serving time.

NUTRIENTS PER SERVING:

Calories: 200, Protein: 7g, Carbohydrate: 36g, Total Fat: 3.5g, (Saturated Fat: 3g), Cholesterol: 0mg, Sodium: 55mg

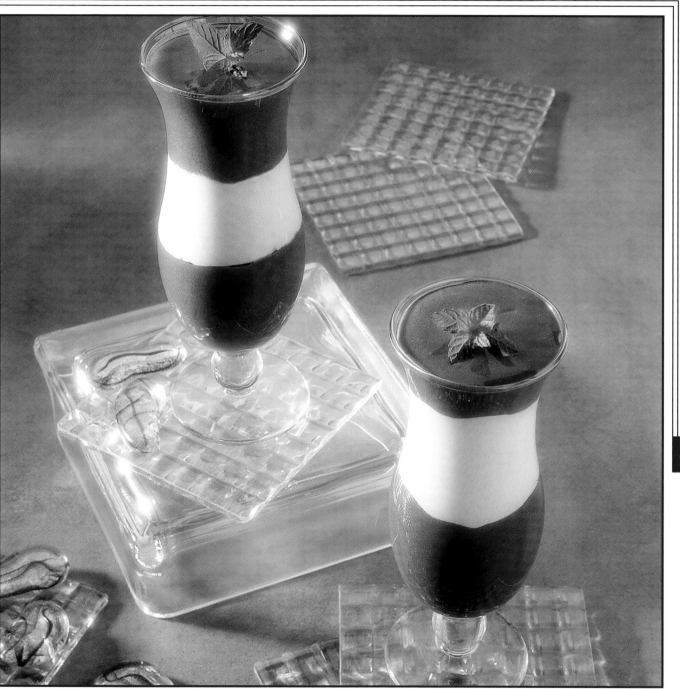

Shamrock Parfaits

3 tablespoons sugar

3 tablespoons HERSHEY'S Cocoa

½ cup hot water

1 (3-inch) stick cinnamon

3 cups nonfat milk

½ teaspoon vanilla extract

HOT COCOA WITH CINNAMON

Makes 4 (7-ounce) servings

Stir together sugar and cocoa in medium saucepan; gradually stir in hot water. Add cinnamon. Cook over medium heat, stirring constantly, until mixture boils; boil and stir 1 minute. Immediately stir in milk; continue cooking and stirring until mixture is hot. Do not boil. Remove from heat; discard cinnamon stick. Stir in vanilla. Beat with rotary beater or whisk until foamy. Serve immediately.

NUTRIENTS PER SERVING:

Calories: 108, Protein: 7g, Carbohydrate: 20g, Total Fat: <1g, (Saturated Fat: <1g), Cholesterol: 3mg, Sodium: 102mg

HERSHEY'S HINT

In 1973, Hershey Foods added nutritional labeling to the wrappers of its candy bars, being the first to do so in the confection industry.

227

Hot Cocoa with Cinnamon

Crushed ice

¾ cup cold nonfat milk

¼ cup sliced fresh strawberries

2 tablespoons HERSHEY'S Syrup

2 tablespoons vanilla ice milk

2 tablespoons club soda

SLIMMING CHOCOBERRY SPLASH

Makes 1 serving

1. Fill two tall glasses with crushed ice.

2. Place all remaining ingredients except club soda in blender container. Cover; blend until smooth. Pour into glasses over crushed ice; add club soda. Garnish as desired. Serve immediately.

VARIATION: Substitute any of the following for strawberries: $1/3$ cup drained canned peach slices, 3 tablespoons frozen raspberries, 2 pineapple slices or $1/4$ cup drained crushed canned pineapple.

NUTRIENTS PER SERVING:

Calories: 210, Protein: 9g, Carbohydrate: 41g, Total Fat: 1.5g, (Saturated Fat: 1g), Cholesterol: 10mg, Sodium: 140mg

Slimming Chocoberry Splash

2½ cups HERSHEY'S Basic
  Cocoa Baking Mix
  (recipe follows)

2 egg whites, slightly beaten

¼ cup (½ stick) corn oil spread
  (60% oil), melted

1 tablespoon water

1 teaspoon vanilla extract

¼ cup sugar

Chocolate Glaze
  (recipe follows)

DOUBLE CHOCOLATE SUGAR COOKIES

Makes 2½ dozen cookies

1. Heat oven to 350°F. Lightly spray cookie sheet with vegetable cooking spray. Prepare Basic Cocoa Baking Mix.

2. Stir together egg whites, corn oil spread, water and vanilla in medium bowl. Stir in Basic Cocoa Baking Mix until well blended. Shape dough into 1-inch balls. Roll in sugar to coat. Place 2 inches apart on prepared cookie sheet. Press balls flat with bottom of glass.

3. Bake 6 to 8 minutes or until set. Cool 5 minutes; remove from cookie sheet to wire racks. Cool completely. Prepare Chocolate Glaze; drizzle over tops of cookies. Let stand until set. Store, covered, at room temperature.

HERSHEY'S BASIC COCOA BAKING MIX: Stir together 4½ cups all-purpose flour, 2¾ cups sugar, 1¼ cups HERSHEY'S Cocoa, 1 tablespoon plus ½ teaspoon baking powder, 1¾ teaspoons salt and 1¼ teaspoons baking soda. Store in airtight container in cool, dry place for up to 1 month. Stir before using. Makes 8 cups mix.

CHOCOLATE GLAZE: In small microwave-safe bowl, place $^1/_4$ cup HERSHEY'S Semi-Sweet Chocolate Chips and $^1/_2$ teaspoon shortening (do not use butter, margarine, spread or oil). Microwave at HIGH (100%) 30 seconds; stir. If necessary, microwave at HIGH an additional 30 seconds or until chips are melted and mixture is smooth when stirred. Use immediately.

NUTRIENTS PER SERVING (1 COOKIE WITH GLAZE):

Calories: 35, Protein: 1g, Carbohydrate: 4g, Total Fat: 2g, (Saturated Fat: 1g), Cholesterol: 0mg, Sodium: 30mg

1 teaspoon unflavored gelatin

1 tablespoon cold water

2 tablespoons boiling water

¼ cup sugar

¼ cup HERSHEY'S Cocoa

1 envelope (1.3 ounces) dry whipped topping mix

½ cup cold lowfat 2% milk

1 teaspoon vanilla extract

SLIMMING CHOCOLATE MOUSSE

Makes 4 servings

1. Sprinkle gelatin over cold water in small cup; let stand 1 minute to soften. Add boiling water; stir until gelatin is completely dissolved. Stir together sugar and cocoa in small bowl. Add gelatin mixture; stir until well blended.

2. Prepare topping mix as directed on package, using $^1/_2$ cup milk and 1 teaspoon vanilla. Beat on high speed of mixer until stiff peaks form. Gradually add chocolate mixture; continue beating on high speed until well blended. Spoon into 4 individual dessert dishes. Cover; refrigerate until firm, about 2 hours.

NUTRIENTS PER SERVING:

Calories: 180, Protein: 5g, Carbohydrate: 30g, Total Fat: 4g, (Saturated Fat: 3g), Cholesterol: 5mg, Sodium: 20mg

1 envelope unflavored gelatin

2 tablespoons cold water

¼ cup boiling water

1 cup sugar

½ cup HERSHEY'S Cocoa

2 cups (1 pint) cold whipping cream

2 teaspoons vanilla extract

1 (6-ounce or 9-ounce) packaged graham cracker crumb crust

Refrigerated whipped light cream in pressurized can

HERSHEY'S MINI KISSES Semi-Sweet *or* Milk Chocolate Baking Pieces

CHOCOLATE MAGIC MOUSSE PIE

Makes 6 to 8 servings

1. Sprinkle gelatin over cold water in small bowl; let stand 2 minutes to soften. Add boiling water; stir until gelatin is completely dissolved and mixture is clear. Cool slightly.

2. Mix sugar and cocoa in large bowl; add whipping cream and vanilla. Beat on medium speed of mixer until stiff, scraping bottom of bowl often, until mixture is stiff. Pour in gelatin mixture; beat until well blended. Spoon into crust. Refrigerate about 3 hours. Garnish with whipped cream and Mini Kisses. Store, covered, in refrigerator.

233

Chocolate Magic Mousse Pie

⅓ cup butter or margarine

⅔ cup sugar

½ cup HERSHEY'S Cocoa

3 eggs

1 cup light corn syrup

¼ teaspoon salt

1 cup chopped pecans

1 unbaked (9-inch) pie crust

Sweetened Whipped Cream
(recipe follows, optional)

Pecan halves (optional)

FUDGEY PECAN PIE

Makes 8 servings

1. Heat oven to 375°F.

2. Melt butter in medium saucepan over low heat. Add sugar and cocoa; stir until well blended. Remove from heat; cool. Beat eggs slightly in medium bowl. Stir in corn syrup and salt. Add cocoa mixture; blend well. Stir in chopped pecans. Pour into unbaked crust.

3. Bake 45 to 50 minutes or until set. Cool completely on wire rack. Cover; let stand about 8 hours before serving. Prepare Sweetened Whipped Cream. Garnish pie with Sweetened Whipped Cream and pecan halves, if desired.

SWEETENED WHIPPED CREAM

½ cup cold whipping cream

1 tablespoon powdered sugar

¼ teaspoon vanilla extract

Stir together whipping cream, powdered sugar and vanilla in small bowl; beat on high speed of mixer until stiff.

FUDGEY MOCHA PECAN PIE: In small bowl or cup, dissolve 1 teaspoon powdered instant coffee in 1 teaspoon hot water; add to pie filling when adding corn syrup and salt.

Fudgey Pecan Pie

1 ⅓ **cups all-purpose flour**

½ **cup powdered sugar**

¼ **cup HERSHEY'S Cocoa *or* HERSHEY'S Dutch Processed Cocoa**

¾ **cup (1 ½ sticks) butter or margarine, softened**

Strawberry Vanilla Filling (page 238)

½ **cup HERSHEY'S Semi-Sweet Chocolate Chips**

1 **tablespoon shortening (do not use butter, margarine, spread or oil)**

Glazed Fruit Topping (page 238)

Fresh fruit, sliced

CHOCOLATE STRAWBERRY FRUIT TART

Makes 12 servings

1. Heat oven to 325°F. Grease and flour 12-inch pizza pan.

2. Stir together flour, powdered sugar and cocoa in medium bowl. With pastry blender or two knives, cut in butter until mixture holds together; press into prepared pan.

3. Bake 10 to 15 minutes or until crust is set. Cool completely.

4. Prepare Strawberry Vanilla Filling; spread over crust to within 1 inch of edge; refrigerate until filling is firm.

5. Place chocolate chips and shortening in small microwave-safe bowl. Microwave at HIGH (100%) 30 seconds; stir. If necessary, microwave at HIGH an additional 15 seconds at a time, stirring after each heating, just until chips are melted when stirred. Spoon chocolate into disposable pastry bag or corner of heavy duty plastic bag; cut off small piece at corner. Squeeze chocolate onto outer edge of filling in decorative design; refrigerate until chocolate is firm.

6. Prepare Glazed Fruit Topping. Arrange fresh fruit over filling; carefully brush prepared topping over fruit. Refrigerate until ready to serve. Cover; refrigerate leftover tart. *continued on page 238*

Chocolate Strawberry Fruit Tart

Chocolate Strawberry Fruit Tart, continued

STRAWBERRY VANILLA FILLING

1⅔ cups (10-ounce package) HERSHEY'S Premier White Chips

¼ cup evaporated milk

1 package (8 ounces) cream cheese, softened

1 teaspoon strawberry extract

2 drops red food color

1. Place white chips and evaporated milk in medium microwave-safe bowl. Microwave at HIGH (100%) 1 minute; stir. If necessary, microwave at HIGH an additional 15 seconds at a time, stirring after each heating, just until chips are melted when stirred.

2. Beat in cream cheese, strawberry extract and red food color.

GLAZED FRUIT TOPPING

¼ teaspoon unflavored gelatin

1 teaspoon cold water

1½ teaspoons cornstarch or arrowroot

¼ cup apricot nectar or orange juice

2 tablespoons sugar

½ teaspoon lemon juice

1. Sprinkle gelatin over water in small cup; let stand 2 minutes to soften.

2. Stir together cornstarch, apricot nectar, sugar and lemon juice in small saucepan. Cook over medium heat, stirring constantly, until mixture is thickened. Remove from heat; immediately stir in gelatin until smooth. Cool slightly.

¾ cup packed light brown sugar

½ cup all-purpose flour

½ teaspoon baking powder

¼ teaspoon ground cinnamon

2 eggs, slightly beaten

1 cup HERSHEY'S Semi-Sweet Chocolate Chips, MINI CHIPS *or* Milk Chocolate Chips

1 cup coarsely chopped walnuts

1 baked (9-inch) pie crust

Spiced Cream (recipe follows)

CHOCOLATE CHIP WALNUT PIE

Makes 1 (9-inch) pie

1. Heat oven to 350°F.

2. Combine brown sugar, flour, baking powder and cinnamon in medium bowl. Add eggs; stir until well blended. Add chocolate chips and walnuts. Pour into baked pie crust.

3. Bake 25 to 30 minutes or until lightly browned and set. Serve slightly warm or at room temperature with Spiced Cream. Refrigerate leftovers.

SPICED CREAM: Combine $1/2$ cup cold whipping cream, 1 tablespoon powdered sugar, $1/4$ teaspoon vanilla extract, $1/4$ teaspoon ground cinnamon and dash ground nutmeg in small bowl; beat until stiff.

⅔ cup HERSHEY'S Semi-Sweet Chocolate Chips

¼ cup milk

1 tablespoon sugar

½ teaspoon vanilla extract

½ cup cold whipping cream

6 single-serve graham cracker crusts (4-ounce package)

Sweetened whipped cream

Sliced fresh fruit, maraschino cherries, chilled cherry pie filling or fresh mint

CREAMY CHOCOLATE TARTS

Makes 6 servings

1. Place chocolate chips, milk and sugar in small microwave-safe bowl. Microwave at HIGH (100%) 1 minute or until milk is hot and chips are melted when stirred. With whisk or rotary beater, beat until mixture is smooth; stir in vanilla. Cool to room temperature.

2. Beat whipping cream until stiff; carefully fold chocolate mixture into whipped cream until blended. Spoon or pipe into crusts. Cover; refrigerate until set. Top with sweetened whipped cream. Garnish as desired.

HERSHEY'S HINT

A tart pan has a shallow, fluted side and a removable bottom. Although round is the most common shape, tart pans are also available in square and rectangular shapes. Tartlet pans, or miniature tart pans, also have fluted sides and are available in a variety of shapes.

Creamy Chocolate Tarts

1¾ cups (10-ounce package) HERSHEY'S MINI KISSES Semi-Sweet *or* Milk Chocolate Baking Pieces, divided

1½ cups miniature marshmallows

⅓ cup milk

1 cup (½ pint) cold whipping cream

1 baked (9-inch) pie crust, cooled

1 can (21 ounces) cherry pie filling, chilled

Whipped topping

EASY MINI KISSES CHOCO-CHERRY PIE

Makes about 8 servings

1. Place 1 cup Mini Kisses, marshmallows and milk in medium microwave-safe bowl. Microwave at HIGH (100%) $1^1/_2$ to 2 minutes or until chocolate is softened and mixture is melted and smooth when stirred; cool completely.

2. Beat whipping cream in small bowl until stiff; fold into chocolate mixture. Spoon into prepared crust. Cover; refrigerate 4 hours or until firm.

3. Garnish top of pie with cherry pie filling, whipped topping and remaining Mini Kisses just before serving. Refrigerate leftover pie.

HERSHEY'S HINT

For optimum volume, beat whipping cream in a deep, narrow bowl. Generally 1 cup of cream will yield 2 cups of whipped cream, so be sure to choose a bowl that will accommodate the increased volume. Do not overbeat or the cream will clump together and form butter.

243

Easy Mini Kisses Choco-Cherry Pie

Tart Shell (page 246)

⅔ **cup HERSHEY'S Semi-Sweet Chocolate Chips**

½ **cup milk, divided**

2 **tablespoons sugar**

½ **teaspoon unflavored gelatin**

1 **tablespoon cold water**

⅔ **cup HERSHEY'S Premier White Chips**

1 **teaspoon vanilla extract**

1 **cup (½ pint) cold whipping cream**

CHOCOLATE & VANILLA SWIRL TART

Makes 8 to 10 servings

1. Prepare Tart Shell.

2. Place chocolate chips, $1/4$ cup milk and sugar in small microwave-safe bowl. Microwave at HIGH (100%) 1 minute; stir. If necessary, microwave at HIGH an additional 15 seconds at a time, stirring after each heating, just until chips are melted when stirred. Cool about 20 minutes.

3. Sprinkle gelatin over water in small cup; let stand 2 minutes to soften. Place white chips and remaining $1/4$ cup milk in second small microwave-safe bowl. Microwave at HIGH 1 minute; stir. Add gelatin mixture and vanilla; stir until gelatin is dissolved. Cool about 20 minutes.

4. Beat whipping cream in small bowl on high speed of mixer until stiff; fold 1 cup whipped cream into vanilla mixture. Fold remaining whipped cream into chocolate mixture. Alternately, spoon chocolate and vanilla mixtures into prepared tart shell; swirl with knife for marbled effect. Refrigerate until firm. Cover; refrigerate leftover tart.

continued on page 246

244

245

Chocolate & Vanilla Swirl Tart

Chocolate & Vanilla Swirl Tart, continued

TART SHELL

> ½ cup (1 stick) butter (do not use margarine), softened
>
> 2 tablespoons sugar
>
> 2 egg yolks
>
> 1 cup all-purpose flour

1. Heat oven to 375°F. Grease bottom and side of fluted 8- or 9-inch tart pan.

2. Beat butter and sugar in small bowl until blended. Add egg yolks; mix well. Stir in flour until mixture is crumbly. Press onto bottom and up side of prepared pan. (If dough is sticky, sprinkle with 1 tablespoon flour.) Prick bottom with fork to prevent puffing. Bake 8 to 10 minutes or until lightly browned. Cool completely.

½ cup (1 stick) butter or margarine, melted

3 cups MOUNDS Sweetened Coconut Flakes

2 tablespoons all-purpose flour

1⅓ cups (8-ounce package) HEATH BITS, divided

½ gallon chocolate ice cream, softened

CHOCOLATE MACAROON HEATH PIE

Makes 6 to 8 servings

1. Heat oven to 375°F. Combine butter, coconut and flour in medium bowl. Press into 9-inch pie plate. Bake at 375°F for 10 minutes or until edge is light golden brown. Cool completely.

2. Set aside ⅓ cup Heath Bits. Combine ice cream and remaining 1 cup Heath Bits. Spread into cooled crust. Sprinkle with ⅓ cup reserved bits. Freeze at least 5 hours. Remove from freezer about 10 minutes before serving.

¾ cup sugar

⅓ cup HERSHEY'S Cocoa

2 tablespoons cornstarch

2 tablespoons all-purpose flour

¼ teaspoon salt

1¾ cups milk

2 egg yolks, slightly beaten

2 tablespoons butter or margarine

¾ teaspoon vanilla extract

⅛ to ¼ teaspoon almond extract

6 single-serve graham cracker crumb crusts (4-ounce package)

Whipped topping

Sliced almonds

CHOCOLATE-ALMOND PUDDING TARTS

Makes 6 servings

1. Stir together sugar, cocoa, cornstarch, flour and salt in medium microwave-safe bowl; gradually add milk and egg yolks, beating with whisk until smooth. Microwave at HIGH (100%) 5 minutes, stirring with whisk after each minute. Continue to microwave at HIGH 1 to 3 minutes or until mixture is smooth and very thick. Stir in butter, vanilla and almond extract. Spoon chocolate mixture equally into crusts. Press plastic wrap directly onto surface.

2. Cool; refrigerate several hours. Just before serving, garnish with whipped topping and sliced almonds. Cover; refrigerate leftover tarts.

½ cup sugar

2 tablespoons butter or margarine

2 tablespoons water

1⅓ cups HERSHEY'S Semi-Sweet Chocolate Chips

2 eggs

⅔ cup all-purpose flour

¼ teaspoon baking soda

¼ teaspoon salt

1 teaspoon vanilla extract

¾ cup chopped nuts (optional)

Fudge Sauce (recipe follows, optional)

Ice cream, any flavor

BROWNIE PIE À LA MODE

Makes 8 to 10 servings

1. Heat oven to 350°F. Grease 9-inch pie plate.

2. Combine sugar, butter and water in medium saucepan. Cook over medium heat, stirring occasionally, just until mixture comes to a boil. Remove from heat. Immediately add chocolate chips; stir until melted. Add eggs; beat with spoon until well blended.

3. Stir together flour, baking soda and salt. Add to chocolate mixture; stir until well blended. Stir in vanilla and nuts, if desired; pour into prepared pie plate.

4. Bake 25 to 30 minutes or until almost set. (Pie will not test done in center.) Cool. Prepare Fudge Sauce, if desired. Top pie with scoops of ice cream and prepared sauce.

FUDGE SAUCE

1 cup HERSHEY'S Semi-Sweet Chocolate Chips

½ cup evaporated milk

¼ cup sugar

1 tablespoon butter or margarine

Combine all ingredients in medium microwave-safe bowl. Microwave at HIGH (100%) 1 minute; stir. If necessary, microwave at HIGH an additional 15 seconds at a time, stirring after each heating, just until chips are melted and mixture is smooth. Cool slightly.

Top to bottom: Hot Cocoa (page 308), Brownie Pie à la Mode

Chocolate Tart Crust
(page 252)

2 tablespoons sugar

2 teaspoons cornstarch

⅛ teaspoon salt

1 cup milk

2 egg yolks, beaten

1 cup HERSHEY'S Semi-Sweet
Chocolate Chips

3 large fresh pears, such as
Bartlett or Anjou

Apricot Glaze (page 252)

CHOCOLATE AND PEAR TART

Makes 12 servings

1. Prepare Chocolate Tart Crust.

2. Combine sugar, cornstarch and salt in heavy medium saucepan; gradually stir in milk. Cook and stir over medium heat until thickened and bubbly. Cook and stir 2 minutes more. Remove from heat; gradually stir about half of hot filling into beaten egg yolks. Pour egg yolk mixture back into hot filling in saucepan; bring to a gentle boil. Cook and stir 2 minutes more. Remove from heat.

3. Immediately add chocolate chips, stirring until chips are melted and mixture is smooth. Pour into Chocolate Tart Crust. Refrigerate several hours or until firm.

4. Core and peel pears; cut into thin slices. Place in circular pattern on top of filling. Immediately prepare Apricot Glaze. Spoon over top of fruit, covering completely. Refrigerate several hours or until firm; remove rim of pan. Serve cold. Cover; refrigerate leftover tart. *continued on page 252*

Chocolate and Pear Tart

Chocolate and Pear Tart, continued

CHOCOLATE TART CRUST: Heat oven to 325°F. Grease and flour 9-inch round tart pan with removable bottom. Stir together ³/₄ cup all-purpose flour, ¹/₄ cup powdered sugar and 1 tablespoon HERSHEY'S Cocoa in small bowl. Beating at low speed of electric mixer, mix in 6 tablespoons chilled margarine until blended and smooth. Press evenly with fingers onto bottom and up side of prepared pan. Bake 10 to 15 minutes; cool.

APRICOT GLAZE

    ¾ teaspoon unflavored gelatin
    2 teaspoons cold water
 2¼ teaspoons cornstarch
    ½ cup apricot nectar
    ¼ cup sugar
    1 teaspoon lemon juice

1. Sprinkle gelatin over cold water in small bowl or cup; let stand several minutes to soften.

2. Combine cornstarch, apricot nectar, sugar and lemon juice in small saucepan; cook over medium heat, stirring constantly, until mixture is thickened. Remove from heat; immediately add gelatin mixture. Stir until smooth.

Macaroon-Nut Crust
(recipe follows)

⅔ cup packed light brown sugar

3 tablespoons all-purpose flour

2 tablespoons cornstarch

½ teaspoon salt

2¼ cups milk

½ cup HERSHEY'S Syrup

3 egg yolks, well beaten

2 tablespoons butter (no substitutes)

1 teaspoon vanilla extract

Sweetened whipped cream (optional)

Maraschino cherries (optional)

1 HERSHEY'S Milk Chocolate Bar (1.55 ounces), broken into pieces (optional)

OUR GAL SUNDAE PIE

Makes 8 servings

1. Prepare Macaroon-Nut Crust.

2. Stir together brown sugar, flour, cornstarch and salt in medium saucepan. Gradually stir in milk, syrup and egg yolks until blended. Cook over medium heat, stirring constantly, until mixture comes to a boil; boil 1 minute, stirring constantly. Remove from heat; stir in butter and vanilla. Pour mixture into prepared crust. Press plastic wrap directly onto surface. Cool on wire rack; refrigerate at least 6 hours.

3. Just before serving, garnish with sweetened whipped cream, maraschino cherries and chocolate bar pieces, if desired. Cover; refrigerate leftover pie.

MACAROON-NUT CRUST

1¼ cups coconut macaroon cookie crumbs (use purchased hard coconut macaroon cookies)

½ cup chopped walnuts

¼ cup (½ stick) butter (no substitutes), melted

1. Heat oven to 350°F.

2. Stir together cookie crumbs, walnuts and butter in medium bowl. Press firmly onto bottom and up side of 9-inch pie plate. Bake 8 to 10 minutes or until lightly browned. Cool completely.

1 package (3 ounces) cream cheese, softened

1 teaspoon lemon juice

1⅔ cups (10-ounce package) REESE'S Peanut Butter Chips, divided

⅔ cup sweetened condensed milk (not evaporated milk)

1 cup (½ pint) cold whipping cream, divided

1 packaged chocolate or graham cracker crumb crust (6 ounces)

1 tablespoon powdered sugar

1 teaspoon vanilla extract

EASY PEANUT BUTTER CHIP PIE

Makes 6 to 8 servings

1. Beat cream cheese and lemon juice in medium bowl until fluffy, about 2 minutes; set aside.

2. Place 1 cup peanut butter chips and sweetened condensed milk in small microwave-safe bowl. Microwave at HIGH (100%) 45 seconds; stir. If necessary, microwave at HIGH an additional 15 seconds at a time, stirring after each heating, until chips are melted and mixture is smooth when stirred.

3. Add warm peanut butter mixture to cream cheese mixture. Beat on medium speed of mixer until blended, about 1 minute. Beat ½ cup whipping cream in another small bowl until stiff; fold into peanut butter mixture. Pour into crust. Cover; refrigerate several hours or overnight until firm.

4. Just before serving, combine remaining ½ cup whipping cream, powdered sugar and vanilla in small bowl. Beat until stiff; spread over filling. Garnish with remaining ⅔ cup peanut butter chips. Cover; refrigerate leftover pie.

Easy Peanut Butter Chip Pie

Chocolate Pastry
(recipe follows)

1 package (3 ounces)
strawberry-flavored gelatin

¾ cup boiling water

1½ cups chopped fresh
strawberries

2 cups frozen non-dairy
whipped topping, thawed

½ cup HERSHEY'S Semi-Sweet
Chocolate Chips

1 teaspoon shortening
(do not use butter,
margarine, spread or oil)

8 whole strawberries

STRAWBERRY CHIFFON PIE

Makes 8 servings

1. Prepare Chocolate Pastry.

2. Dissolve gelatin in boiling water in medium bowl; cool slightly. Crush strawberries or purée to equal $3/4$ cup. Stir strawberry purée into gelatin mixture; refrigerate until partially set (consistency of unbeaten egg whites). Fold whipped topping into strawberry mixture. Spoon into prepared crust. Refrigerate 2 to 3 hours or until set.

3. Line tray with wax paper. Place chocolate chips and shortening in small microwave-safe bowl. Microwave at HIGH (100%) 1 minute; stir. If necessary, microwave at HIGH an additional 15 seconds at a time, stirring after each heating, just until chips are melted when stirred. Dip whole strawberries into melted chocolate; place on prepared tray. Refrigerate, uncovered, about 30 minutes or until chocolate is firm. Just before serving, garnish pie with chocolate-covered strawberries. Cover; refrigerate leftover pie.

Chocolate Pastry

1 ¼ **cups all-purpose flour**
¼ **cup sugar**
3 **tablespoons HERSHEY'S Cocoa**
¼ **teaspoon salt**
⅓ **cup vegetable oil**
3 **tablespoons cold water**

1. Stir together flour, sugar, cocoa and salt in medium bowl. Pour oil into measuring cup; add water. Do not stir. Pour liquid over flour mixture; stir lightly with fork until well blended. (If mixture is too dry, add 1 to 2 teaspoons additional cold water.)

2. With hands, shape mixture into ball. Place between two pieces of wax paper; roll into 12-inch circle. Peel off top sheet of paper. Gently invert pastry over 9-inch pie plate; peel off paper. Fit pastry into pie plate. Fold under extra pastry around edge; flute edge. With fork, prick bottom and side of crust thoroughly. Refrigerate about 30 minutes.

3. Meanwhile, heat oven to 450°F. Bake 10 minutes. Cool completely.

½ cup HERSHEY'S Cocoa

1¼ cups sugar

⅓ cup cornstarch

¼ teaspoon salt

3 cups milk

3 tablespoons butter or margarine

1½ teaspoons vanilla extract

1 baked 9-inch pie crust or graham cracker crumb crust, cooled

HERSHEY'S COCOA CREAM PIE

Makes 6 to 8 servings

1. Stir together cocoa, sugar, cornstarch and salt in medium saucepan. Gradually add milk, stirring until smooth. Cook over medium heat, stirring constantly, until mixture comes to a boil; boil 1 minute. Remove from heat; stir in butter and vanilla.

2. Pour into prepared crust. Press plastic wrap directly onto surface. Cool to room temperature. Refrigerate 6 to 8 hours. Garnish as desired. Cover; refrigerate leftover pie.

HERSHEY'S HINT

Use the pan size specified in each recipe and prepare it as stated. The wrong size pan may cause a burned bottom or edges or a sunken middle.

Hershey's Cocoa Cream Pie

1 teaspoon unflavored gelatin

1 tablespoon cold water

2 tablespoons boiling water

½ cup sugar

⅓ cup HERSHEY'S Cocoa *or* HERSHEY'S Dutch Processed Cocoa

1 cup (½ pint) cold whipping cream

1 teaspoon vanilla extract

1 baked (8- or 9-inch) pie crust, cooled

Mint Cream Topping (recipe follows)

CHOCOLATE MINT MOUSSE PIE

Makes 6 to 8 servings

1. Sprinkle gelatin over cold water in small cup; let stand 2 minutes to soften. Add boiling water; stir until gelatin is completely dissolved and mixture is clear. Cool slightly, about 5 minutes.

2. Meanwhile, stir together sugar and cocoa in medium bowl; add whipping cream and vanilla. Beat on medium speed of mixer until stiff, scraping bottom of bowl occasionally. Add gelatin mixture; beat just until blended. Pour into prepared crust.

3. Prepare Mint Cream Topping; spread over filling. Refrigerate about 2 hours. Garnish as desired. Cover; refrigerate leftover pie.

MINT CREAM TOPPING

1 cup (½ pint) cold whipping cream

2 tablespoons powdered sugar

¼ to ½ teaspoon peppermint extract

Green food color

Beat whipping cream, powdered sugar, peppermint extract and several drops green food color in medium bowl on medium speed of mixer until stiff.

Top to bottom: Frosty Chocolate Chip Pie (page 262), Chocolate Mint Mousse Pie, Strawberry Chiffon Pie (page 256)

1 cup HERSHEY'S Semi-Sweet
    Chocolate Chips

⅓ cup milk

1 package (3 ounces) cream
    cheese, softened

2½ cups frozen non-dairy
    whipped topping, thawed

1 baked (8-inch) pie crust,
    cooled, or packaged
    crumb crust (6 ounces)

Additional whipped topping

Fresh fruit

FROSTY CHOCOLATE CHIP PIE

Makes 6 to 8 servings

1. Place chocolate chips and milk in medium microwave-safe bowl. Microwave at HIGH (100%) 1½ minutes; stir. If necessary, microwave at HIGH an additional 15 seconds at a time, stirring after each heating, just until chips are melted when stirred.

2. Beat in cream cheese with whisk or spoon until mixture is well blended and smooth. Cool just to room temperature. Gradually fold 2½ cups whipped topping into chocolate mixture; spoon into prepared crust.

3. Cover; freeze until firm. Garnish with additional whipped topping and fruit. Freeze leftover pie.

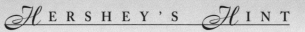

HERSHEY'S HINT

When storing pies, remember that any type made with eggs or dairy products, such as chiffon, cream and custard pies, should always be kept refrigerated. Fruit pies may be stored at room temperature for a day or two. After that, they should also be refrigerated.

1 ⅓ cups **HERSHEY'S MINI KISSES Semi-Sweet** *or* **Milk Chocolate Baking Pieces, divided**

2 tablespoons milk

1 packaged crumb crust (6 ounces)

1 package (8 ounces) Neufchâtel cheese (⅓ less fat), softened

¾ cup sugar

1 cup **REESE'S Creamy** *or* **Crunchy Peanut Butter**

3½ cups (8 ounces) frozen non-dairy whipped topping, thawed

REESE'S PEANUT BUTTER 'N' CHOCOLATE PIE

Makes 8 servings

1. Place ²/₃ cup Mini Kisses and milk in small microwave-safe bowl. Microwave at HIGH (100%) 30 to 45 seconds or just until melted and smooth when stirred; spread evenly onto bottom of crust. Cover; refrigerate.

2. Beat Neufchâtel cheese in medium bowl until smooth; gradually beat in sugar. Stir in peanut butter and whipped topping until blended; spoon evenly into crust over chocolate mixture. Cover; refrigerate until set, at least 4 hours.

3. Place remaining ²/₃ cup Mini Kisses around edge of filling just before serving. Serve cold; cover and refrigerate leftover pie.

Prep Time: 20 minutes
Cook Time: 30 seconds
Chill Time: 4 hours

1 package (3 ounces) cream cheese, softened

¼ cup sugar

1 teaspoon vanilla extract

½ cup HERSHEY'S Syrup

1 cup (½ pint) cold whipping cream

1 packaged crumb crust (6 ounces)

Sliced fresh fruit (optional)

Chocolate curls (optional)

COOL 'N CREAMY CHOCOLATE PIE

Makes 6 to 8 servings

1. Beat cream cheese, sugar and vanilla in medium bowl until well blended. Gradually add syrup, beating until smooth. Beat whipping cream until stiff. Carefully fold into chocolate mixture. Pour into crust.

2. Cover; freeze until firm, about 3 hours. Just before serving, garnish with fresh fruit and chocolate curls, if desired.

HERSHEY'S HINT

To soften cream cheese quickly, remove from wrapper and place in medium microwave-safe bowl. Microwave at MEDIUM (50%) 1½ to 2 minutes or until slightly softened, turning bowl after 1 minute.

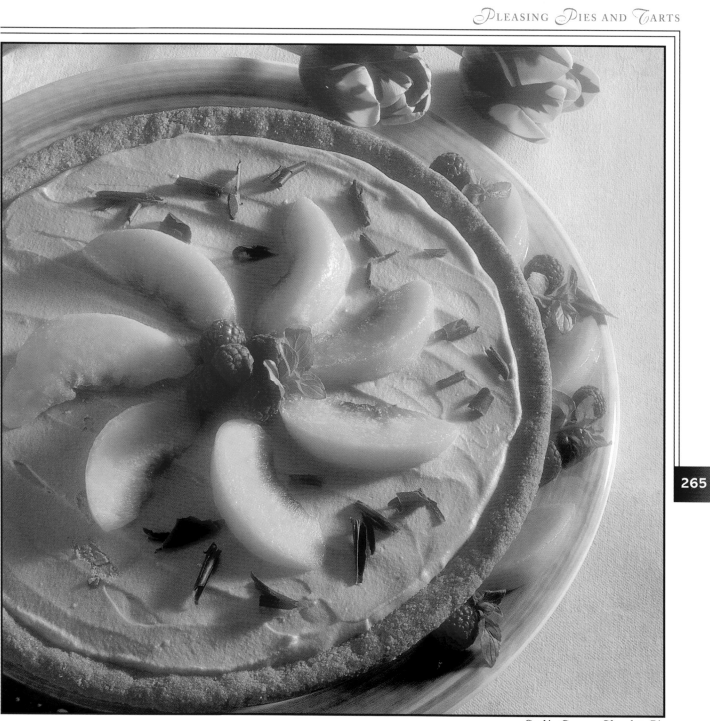

Cool'n Creamy Chocolate Pie

2 eggs

1 cup sugar

½ cup (1 stick) butter or margarine, melted

½ cup all-purpose flour

⅓ cup HERSHEY'S Cocoa

¼ teaspoon salt

1 teaspoon vanilla extract

½ cup chopped nuts (optional)

Ice cream

Hot Fudge Sauce (recipe follows)

FUDGE BROWNIE PIE

Makes 6 to 8 servings

1. Heat oven to 350°F. Lightly grease 8-inch pie plate.

2. Beat eggs in small bowl; blend in sugar and melted butter. Stir together flour, cocoa and salt; add to butter mixture. Stir in vanilla and nuts, if desired. Pour into prepared pie plate.

3. Bake 25 to 30 minutes or until almost set. (Pie will not test done in center.) Cool; cut into wedges. Prepare Hot Fudge Sauce. Serve topped with scoop of ice cream and drizzled with Hot Fudge Sauce.

HOT FUDGE SAUCE

Makes about 1³/₄ cups sauce

¾ cup sugar

½ cup HERSHEY'S Cocoa

½ cup plus 2 tablespoons (5-ounce can) evaporated milk

⅓ cup light corn syrup

⅓ cup butter or margarine

1 teaspoon vanilla extract

Stir together sugar and cocoa in small saucepan; blend in evaporated milk and corn syrup. Cook over medium heat, stirring constantly, until mixture boils; boil and stir 1 minute. Remove from heat; stir in butter and vanilla. Serve warm.

Fudge Brownie Pie

2 eggs

1 teaspoon vanilla extract

1 cup sugar

½ cup (1 stick) butter or margarine, melted

½ cup all-purpose flour

⅓ cup HERSHEY'S Cocoa

¼ teaspoon salt

⅔ cup REESE'S Peanut Butter Chips

1 packaged butter-flavored crumb crust (6 ounces)

Peanut Butter Sauce (recipe follows)

Vanilla ice cream

Fudgey Peanut Butter Chip Brownie Pie

Makes 8 servings

1. Heat oven to 350°F.

2. Lightly beat eggs and vanilla in small bowl; blend in sugar and butter. Stir together flour, cocoa and salt. Add to egg mixture; beat until blended. Stir in peanut butter chips. Place crust on baking sheet; pour chocolate mixture into crust.

3. Bake 45 to 50 minutes or until set; cool completely on wire rack. Prepare Peanut Butter Sauce; serve over pie and ice cream.

Peanut Butter Sauce

1 cup REESE'S Peanut Butter Chips

⅓ cup milk

¼ cup whipping cream

¼ teaspoon vanilla extract

Combine peanut butter chips, milk and whipping cream in small saucepan over low heat. Cook, stirring constantly, until chips are melted and mixture is smooth. Remove from heat; stir in vanilla. Serve warm.

1 cup sugar

½ cup HERSHEY'S Cocoa

3 tablespoons cornstarch

¼ teaspoon salt

2 cups cold milk

2 egg yolks, beaten

1 tablespoon butter

1 teaspoon vanilla extract

1 baked (8-inch) pastry shell, cooled

Sweetened whipped cream

SILKY COCOA CREAM PIE

Makes 8 servings

1. Mix sugar, cocoa, cornstarch and salt in saucepan. Gradually stir in milk. Cook over medium heat, stirring constantly, until mixture is thickened and bubbly. Boil 1 minute; remove from heat.

2. Gradually stir about half of the hot filling into yolks. Return all to saucepan; heat to gentle boil. Cook and stir 1 minute. Remove from heat; stir in butter and vanilla. Pour into crust.

3. Press plastic wrap directly onto pie surface. Cool. Refrigerate 3 to 6 hours or until set. Remove plastic wrap; garnish with sweetened whipped cream. Cover; refrigerate leftover pie.

1 package (4-serving size) chocolate cook & serve pudding and pie filling mix*

1 cup HERSHEY'S MINI CHIPS Semi-Sweet Chocolate

6 single serve graham cracker crusts (4-ounce package)

Whipped topping

Additional MINI CHIPS Semi-Sweet Chocolate

*Do not use instant pudding mix.

MINI CHOCOLATE PIES

Makes 6 servings

1. Prepare pudding and pie filling mix as directed on package; remove from heat. Immediately add 1 cup Mini Chips; stir until melted. Cool 5 minutes, stirring occasionally.

2. Pour filling into crusts; press plastic wrap directly onto surface. Refrigerate several hours or until firm. Garnish with whipped topping and Mini Chips.

Prep Time: 5 minutes
Cook Time: 10 minutes
Cool Time: 5 minutes
Chill Time: 2 hours

---

*H*ERSHEY'S *H*INT

When cutting cream pies, the slices will cut better if the knife is wiped with a damp cloth or paper towel between cuts.

271

Mini Chocolate Pies

Chocolate Petal Crust
(recipe follows)

1 ⅓ cups HERSHEY'S MINI
KISSES Milk Chocolate
Baking Pieces

⅓ cup milk

1½ cups miniature marshmallows

1 cup (½ pint) cold whipping
cream

Sweetened whipped cream

Additional HERSHEY'S MINI
KISSES

HERSHEY'S Chocolate Pie with Chocolate Petal Crust

Makes 8 servings

1. Prepare Chocolate Petal Crust.

2. Microwave Mini Kisses with milk in large microwave-safe bowl at HIGH (100%) 1 minute; stir until well blended. Stir in marshmallows. Microwave at HIGH 30 seconds; stir. If necessary, microwave at HIGH an additional 15 seconds at a time, stirring after each heating until marshmallows are melted. Cool to room temperature.

3. Beat whipping cream in medium bowl until stiff; carefully fold into chocolate mixture. Spoon into prepared crust. Refrigerate until firm, about 4 hours. Garnish with sweetened whipped cream and Mini Kisses. Cover; refrigerate leftover pie.

CHOCOLATE PETAL CRUST

Makes 1 (9-inch) crust

> ½ cup (1 stick) butter or margarine, softened
> 1 cup sugar
> 1 egg
> 1 teaspoon vanilla extract
> 1 ¼ cups all-purpose flour
> ½ cup HERSHEY'S Cocoa
> ¾ teaspoon baking soda
> ¼ teaspoon salt

1. Beat butter, sugar, egg and vanilla in large bowl until fluffy. Stir together flour, cocoa, baking soda and salt; beat into butter mixture. Shape soft dough into two rolls, about 7¹/₂ inches long. Wrap each roll in wax paper or plastic wrap; refrigerate several hours or overnight.

2. Heat oven to 375°F. Grease 9-inch pie plate.

3. Cut one roll into ¹/₈-inch-thick slices. Place on bottom and up side of prepared pie plate, edges touching. (Spaces between slices of dough in crust fill in during baking.)

4. Bake 8 to 10 minutes. Cool completely.

NOTE: Recipe yields enough dough for 2 crusts. Remaining roll of dough may be frozen up to 6 weeks for later use.

1¾ (10-ounce) package SKOR *or* HEATH Bits 'O Brickle, divided

1 tablespoon water

1 package (8 ounces) cream cheese, softened

½ cup plus 1 tablespoon HERSHEY'S Semi-Sweet Chocolate Chips, divided

1 cup (½ pint) cold whipping cream, divided

1 baked (9-inch) pie crust, cooled

½ teaspoon shortening (do not use butter, margarine, spread or oil)

CHOCOLATE TRUFFLE TOFFEE MOUSSE PIE

Makes 6 to 8 servings

1. Combine 1 cup toffee bits and water in small saucepan. Cook over medium heat, stirring constantly, until chocolate is melted. Gradually beat toffee mixture into cream cheese in medium bowl. Refrigerate 20 minutes.

2. Place ½ cup semi-sweet chocolate chips and 3 tablespoons whipping cream in small microwave-safe bowl. Microwave at HIGH (100%) 1 minute; stir. If necessary, microwave an additional 10 seconds or until chocolate is melted and mixture is smooth when stirred. Spread chocolate mixture onto bottom of baked crust; refrigerate.

3. Beat remaining whipped cream in small bowl until stiff; gradually stir into toffee mixture, blending well. Gently stir in ½ cup toffee bits. Spread over chocolate layer. Cover; refrigerate until well chilled, about 4 hours.

4. Shortly before serving, place remaining 1 tablespoon chocolate chips and shortening in small microwave-safe bowl. Microwave at HIGH 1 minute or until chocolate is melted and smooth when stirred; drizzle over top of pie. Garnish with remaining toffee bits. Refrigerate until drizzle is set. Cover; refrigerate leftover pie.

1 envelope unflavored gelatin

1¾ cups milk, divided

⅔ cup sugar

6 tablespoons HERSHEY'S Cocoa

1 tablespoon light corn syrup

2 tablespoons butter (do not use margarine, spread or oil)

¾ teaspoon vanilla extract

1 cup (½ pint) cold whipping cream

1 baked 9-inch pie crust or crumb crust

CHOCOLATE BAVARIAN PIE

Makes 6 to 8 servings

1. Sprinkle gelatin over 1 cup milk in medium saucepan; let stand 2 minutes to soften.

2. Stir together sugar and cocoa. Add to mixture in saucepan. Add corn syrup. Cook, stirring constantly, until mixture comes to a boil. Remove from heat. Add butter; stir until melted. Stir in remaining 3/4 cup milk and vanilla. Pour into large bowl. Cool; refrigerate until almost set.

3. Beat whipping cream in small bowl on high speed of mixer until stiff. Beat chocolate mixture on medium speed of mixer until smooth. On low speed, add half the whipped cream to chocolate mixture, beating just until blended. Pour into prepared crust. Refrigerate 3 hours or until firm. Just before serving, garnish with remaining whipped cream. Cover; refrigerate leftover pie.

Tasty Treats

⅔ cup nonfat dry milk powder

⅔ cup sugar

¼ cup HERSHEY'S Cocoa

2 tablespoons cornstarch

4 cups (1 quart) nonfat milk, divided

¼ teaspoon freshly grated orange peel

⅛ teaspoon orange extract

Orange Cups (directions follow, optional)

Additional freshly grated orange peel (optional)

TROPICAL CHOCOLATE ORANGE ICE MILK

Makes 8 servings

1. Stir together milk powder, sugar, cocoa and cornstarch in medium saucepan. Gradually stir in 2 cups nonfat milk. Cook over medium heat, stirring constantly, until mixture is smooth and slightly thickened, about 5 minutes.

2. Remove from heat. Stir in remaining 2 cups milk, $1/4$ teaspoon orange peel and orange extract. Cover; refrigerate several hours until cold.

3. Pour mixture into 2-quart ice cream freezer container. Freeze according to manufacturer's directions. Before serving, let stand at room temperature until slightly softened. Prepare Orange Cups. Scoop $1/2$ cup ice milk into each Orange Cup or 8 individual dessert dishes. Garnish with additional orange peel, if desired.

ORANGE CUPS: Cut about 1-inch slice from tops of 8 oranges; discard. Using sharp knife, cut out and remove small triangle-shaped notches around tops of oranges to make zig-zag pattern. Scoop out pulp; reserve for other uses.

Tropical Chocolate Orange Ice Milk

1⅓ cups REESE'S Crunchy
      Peanut Butter

¾ cup (1½ sticks) butter or
      margarine, softened

3 cups powdered sugar

2 cups (12-ounce package)
      HERSHEY'S Semi-Sweet
      Chocolate Chips

1 tablespoon shortening
      (do not use butter,
      margarine, spread or oil)

HERSHEY'S BUCKEYES

Makes about 5 dozen candies

1. Beat peanut butter and butter in large bowl until blended. Gradually add powdered sugar, beating until well blended. Cover; refrigerate until firm enough to shape, about 30 minutes.

2. Shape into 1-inch balls. Cover; refrigerate until firm, about 1 hour.

3. Place chocolate chips and shortening in medium microwave-safe bowl. Microwave at HIGH (100%) 1½ minutes; stir. If necessary, microwave at HIGH an additional 15 seconds at a time, stirring after each heating, just until chips are melted when stirred.

4. Dip each ball into chocolate mixture, coating ¾ of ball. Place on wax paper, uncoated side up. Let stand until chocolate hardens. Store, covered, in refrigerator.

Prep Time: 30 minutes
Chill Time: 1½ hours
Cook Time: 1½ minutes
Cool Time: 1 hour

1⅔ cups (10-ounce package) REESE'S Peanut Butter Chips

2 tablespoons vegetable oil

2 teaspoons vanilla extract, divided

2 cups (12-ounce package) HERSHEY'S Semi-Sweet Chocolate Chips

2 cups light corn syrup

1⅓ cups packed light brown sugar

12 cups crisp rice cereal, divided

DOUBLE-DECKER CEREAL TREATS

Makes about 6 dozen pieces

1. Line $15\frac{1}{2}\times10\frac{1}{2}\times1$-inch jelly-roll pan with foil, extending foil over edges of pan.

2. Place peanut butter chips, oil and 1 teaspoon vanilla in large bowl. Place chocolate chips and remaining 1 teaspoon vanilla in second large bowl. Stir together corn syrup and brown sugar in large saucepan; cook over medium heat, stirring constantly, until mixture comes to full rolling boil. Remove from heat. Immediately pour half of hot mixture into each reserved bowl; stir each mixture until chips are melted and mixture is smooth. Immediately stir 6 cups rice cereal into each of the two mixtures. Spread peanut butter mixture into prepared pan; spread chocolate mixture over top of peanut butter layer.

3. Cool completely. Use foil to lift treats out of pan; peel off foil. Cut treats into bars. Store in tightly covered container in cool, dry place.

2 cups (11.5 ounce package)
HERSHEY'S Milk Chocolate
Chips
¾ cup coarsely chopped salted
or unsalted cashews
¾ cup coarsely chopped salted
or unsalted macadamia
nuts
½ cup (1 stick) butter, softened
½ cup sugar
2 tablespoons light corn syrup

CASHEW MACADAMIA CRUNCH

Makes about 1½ pounds

1. Line 9-inch square pan with foil, extending foil over edges of pan. Grease foil. Cover bottom of prepared pan with chocolate chips.

2. Combine cashews, macadamia nuts, butter, sugar and corn syrup in large heavy skillet; cook over low heat, stirring constantly, until butter is melted and sugar is dissolved. Increase heat to medium; cook, stirring constantly, until mixture begins to cling together and turns golden brown.

3. Pour mixture over chocolate chips in pan, spreading evenly. Cool. Refrigerate until chocolate is firm. Remove from pan; peel off foil. Break into pieces. Store tightly covered in cool, dry place.

Prep Time: 30 minutes
Cook Time: 10 minutes
Cool Time: 40 minutes
Chill Time: 3 hours

Cashew Macadamia Crunch

1 cup HERSHEY'S Semi-Sweet
    Chocolate Chips

½ cup HERSHEY'S Premier
    White Chips

1 tablespoon shortening
    (do not use butter,
    margarine, spread or oil)

Fresh strawberries, rinsed
    and patted dry (about
    2 pints)

CREAMY CHOCOLATE DIPPED STRAWBERRIES

Makes about 3 dozen dipped berries

1. Line tray with wax paper.

2. Place chocolate chips, white chips and shortening in medium microwave-safe bowl. Microwave at HIGH (100%) 1 minute; stir. If necessary, microwave at HIGH an additional 15 seconds at a time, stirring after each heating, just until chips are melted when stirred. Holding top, dip bottom two-thirds of each strawberry into melted mixture; shake gently to remove excess. Place on prepared tray.

3. Refrigerate about 1 hour or until coating is firm. Cover; refrigerate leftover dipped berries. For best results, use within 24 hours.

1 cup HERSHEY'S Milk Chocolate Chips

1 teaspoon shortening (do not use butter, margarine, spread or oil)

1 cup broken pecans or walnuts

CHOCOLATE NUT CLUSTERS

Makes 14 to 16 candies

1. Place chocolate chips and shortening in medium microwave-safe bowl. Microwave at HIGH (100%) 1 minute; stir. If necessary, microwave at HIGH an additional 15 seconds at a time, stirring after each heating, just until chips are melted and mixture is smooth when stirred. Stir in nuts. Spoon heaping teaspoons into 1-inch paper candy cups or paper-lined small muffin cups, filling each cup about $1/2$ full.

2. Refrigerate until firm. Peel off paper cups. Store in tightly covered container in refrigerator.

HERSHEY'S HINT

Pecans are native to the United States and are grown in the South and Southwest. Next to the peanut, it is the most popular nut in the United States.

2 cups vanilla wafer crumbs
(about 60 wafers, crushed)

1 cup finely chopped almonds

⅓ cup HERSHEY'S Cocoa

1 can (14 ounces) sweetened
condensed milk (not
evaporated milk)

1 package (8 ounces) dried
apricots, chopped

½ cup chopped candied
cherries

¼ teaspoon almond extract

2 cups (11.5-ounce package)
HERSHEY'S Milk Chocolate
Chips

4 teaspoons shortening (do
not use butter, margarine,
spread or oil)

CHOCOLATE-COVERED ALMOND APRICOT TASSIES

Makes about 6 dozen candies

1. Line small muffin cups ($1^3/4$ inches in diameter) with paper bake cups.

2. Combine crumbs, almonds and cocoa in large bowl. Add sweetened condensed milk, apricots, cherries and almond extract; mix well. Refrigerate 30 minutes. Roll mixture into 1-inch balls; press into prepared muffin cups.

3. Place chocolate chips and shortening in medium microwave-safe bowl. Microwave at HIGH (100%) $1^1/2$ minutes; stir. If necessary, microwave at HIGH an additional 15 seconds at a time, stirring after each heating, just until chips are melted when stirred. Spoon about 1 teaspoon melted chocolate over each filled cup. Refrigerate until chocolate is set. Store, covered, in refrigerator.

TIP: When melting chocolate, even a small amount of moisture may cause it to "seize," or become stiff and grainy. Chocolate can sometimes be returned to melting consistency by adding 1 teaspoon solid shortening (do not use butter, margarine, spread or oil) for every 2 ounces of chocolate and reheating it.

Prep Time: 40 minutes
Cook Time: $1^1/2$ minutes
Chill Time: 1 hour

Chocolate-Covered Almond Apricot Tassies

2 cups sugar

½ cup (1 stick) butter or margarine

½ cup milk

⅓ cup HERSHEY'S Cocoa

⅔ cup REESE'S Crunchy Peanut Butter

3 cups quick-cooking rolled oats

½ cup chopped peanuts (optional)

2 teaspoons vanilla extract

FUDGEY COCOA NO-BAKE TREATS

Makes about 4 dozen pieces

1. Place piece of wax paper or foil on tray or cookie sheet. Combine sugar, butter, milk and cocoa in medium saucepan.

2. Cook over medium heat, stirring constantly, until mixture comes to a rolling boil.

3. Remove from heat; cool 1 minute.

4. Add peanut butter, oats, peanuts, if desired, and vanilla; stir to mix well. Quickly drop mixture by heaping teaspoons onto wax paper or foil. Cool completely. Store in cool, dry place.

Prep Time: 20 minutes
Cook Time: 5 minutes
Cool Time: 30 minutes

2 cups (12-ounce package)
    HERSHEY'S Semi-Sweet
    Chocolate Chips

¼ cup butter or margarine

2 tablespoons shortening

3 cups miniature
    marshmallows

½ cup coarsely chopped nuts

EASY ROCKY ROAD

Makes 16 squares

1. Grease 8-inch square pan.

2. Place chocolate chips, butter and shortening in large microwave-safe bowl. Microwave at HIGH (100%) 1 to 1½ minutes or just until chocolate chips are melted and mixture is smooth when stirred. Add marshmallows and nuts; blend well.

3. Spread evenly in prepared pan. Cover; refrigerate until firm. Cut into 2-inch squares. Cover; store in refrigerator.

HERSHEY'S HINT

The tools needed for measuring dry ingredients include a set of four metal or plastic dry measures (1 cup, ½ cup, ⅓ cup and ¼ cup) and a set of measuring spoons (1 tablespoon, 1 teaspoon, ½ teaspoon, ¼ teaspoon and sometimes ⅛ teaspoon).

½ cup whipping cream

3 tablespoons butter

1 cup HERSHEY'S Semi-Sweet Chocolate Chips

1 teaspoon vanilla extract

White Coating (recipe follows)

WHITE COATED CHOCOLATE TRUFFLES

Makes about 2 dozen truffles

1. Combine whipping cream and butter in medium saucepan. Cook over medium heat, stirring constantly, just until mixture begins to boil; remove from heat. Add chocolate chips, stirring until completely melted; continue stirring until mixture cools and thickens slightly. Stir in vanilla. Pour into shallow glass dish. Cover; refrigerate until firm.

2. To form truffles, with spoon, scoop mixture; shape into 1-inch balls. Place on wax paper-lined tray. Cover; refrigerate until firm.

3. Prepare White Coating. Dip truffles in coating; refrigerate. Serve well chilled. Store in tightly covered container in refrigerator.

WHITE COATING: Combine $1^2/_3$ cups (10-ounce package) HERSHEY'S Premier White Chips with 1 tablespoon shortening (do not use butter, margarine, spread or oil) in small microwave-safe bowl. Microwave at HIGH (100%) 1 minute or just until chips are melted when stirred. (Coating works best for dipping between 85° and 90°F. If coating goes below 85°F, place bowl in larger bowl containing warm water; stir until temperature reaches 85°F. Be careful not to get any water into coating mixture.)

Prep Time: 1 hour
Cook Time: 3 minutes
Cool Time: 10 minutes
Chill Time: 5 hours

PEANUT BUTTER 'N' CHOCOLATE CHIPS SNACK MIX

Makes 14 cups snack mix

6 cups bite-size crisp corn, rice or wheat squares cereal

3 cups miniature pretzels

2 cups toasted oat cereal rings

1 cup raisins or dried fruit bits

1 cup HERSHEY'S Semi-Sweet Chocolate Chips

1 cup REESE'S Peanut Butter Chips

Stir together all ingredients in large bowl. Store in airtight container at room temperature.

10 to 12 medium apples, stems removed

10 to 12 wooden ice cream sticks

1 cup HERSHEY'S Semi-Sweet Chocolate Chips

1⅔ cups (10-ounce package) REESE'S Peanut Butter Chips, divided

¼ cup plus 2 tablespoons shortening (do not use butter, margarine, spread or oil), divided

CHOCOLATE & PEANUT BUTTER DIPPED APPLES

Makes 10 to 12 coated apples

1. Line tray with wax paper. Wash apples; dry thoroughly. Insert wooden stick into each apple; place on prepared tray.

2. Place chocolate chips, $2/3$ cup peanut butter chips and $1/4$ cup shortening in medium microwave-safe bowl. Microwave at HIGH (100%) 1 minute; stir. If necessary, microwave at HIGH an additional 30 seconds at a time, stirring after each heating, just until chips are melted when stirred. Dip bottom three-fourths of each apple into mixture. Twirl and gently shake to remove excess; return to prepared tray.

3. Place remaining 1 cup peanut butter chips and remaining 2 tablespoons shortening in small microwave-safe bowl. Microwave at HIGH 30 seconds; stir. If necessary, microwave at HIGH an additional 15 seconds at a time, stirring after each heating, just until chips are melted when stirred. Spoon over top section of each apple, allowing to drip down sides. Store in refrigerator.

291

Chocolate & Peanut Butter Dipped Apples

4 cups sugar

1 jar (7 ounces) marshmallow creme

1½ cups (12-ounce can) evaporated milk

1 cup REESE'S Creamy *or* Crunchy Peanut Butter

1 tablespoon butter or margarine

1 cup HERSHEY'S Semi-Sweet Chocolate Chips *or* HERSHEY'S Milk Chocolate Chips

CHOCOLATE CHIP PEANUT BUTTER FUDGE

Makes about 8 dozen pieces or 3½ pounds

1. Line 13×9×2-inch pan with foil, extending foil over edges of pan. Lightly butter foil.

2. Stir together sugar, marshmallow creme, evaporated milk, peanut butter and butter in heavy 4-quart saucepan. Cook over medium heat, stirring constantly, until mixture comes to full rolling boil; boil and stir 5 minutes. Remove from heat. Immediately add chocolate chips; stir until smooth. Pour into prepared pan; cool until firm.

3. Use foil to lift fudge out of pan; peel off foil. Cut fudge into squares. Store in tightly covered container in cool, dry place.

NOTE: For best results, do not double this recipe.

Prep Time: 15 minutes
Cook Time: 15 minutes
Cool Time: 3 hours

3 bars (1 ounce each)
HERSHEY'S Unsweetened
Baking Chocolate

¼ cup (½ stick) butter

½ cup sweetened condensed
milk (not evaporated milk)

¾ cup granulated sugar

¼ cup water

1 tablespoon light corn syrup

1 teaspoon vanilla extract

2 cups MOUNDS Sweetened
Coconut Flakes

1 cup chopped nuts

Powdered sugar

CHOCOLATE COCONUT BALLS

Makes about 4 dozen candies

1. Melt chocolate and butter in large heavy saucepan over very low heat. Add sweetened condensed milk; stir to blend. Remove from heat.

2. Stir together granulated sugar, water and corn syrup in small saucepan. Cook over medium heat, stirring constantly, until sugar is dissolved. Cook, without stirring, until mixture reaches 250°F on candy thermometer or until a small amount of syrup, when dropped into very cold water, forms a firm ball which does not flatten when removed from water. (Bulb of candy thermometer should not rest on bottom of saucepan.) Remove from heat; stir into chocolate mixture. Add vanilla, coconut and nuts; stir until well blended.

3. Refrigerate about 30 minutes or until firm enough to handle. Shape into 1-inch balls; roll in powdered sugar. Store tightly covered in cool, dry place.

NOTE: For best results, do not double this recipe.

Prep Time: 25 minutes
Cook Time: 20 minutes
Chill Time: 30 minutes

1 cup REESE'S Peanut Butter
  Chips
1 can (14 ounces) sweetened
  condensed milk (not
  evaporated milk), divided
1 teaspoon vanilla extract,
  divided
1 cup HERSHEY'S Semi-Sweet
  Chocolate Chips

CREAMY DOUBLE DECKER FUDGE

Makes about 4 dozen pieces or 1 1/2 pounds

1. Line 8-inch square pan with foil.

2. Place peanut butter chips and $^2/_3$ cup sweetened condensed milk in small microwave-safe bowl. Microwave at HIGH (100%) 1 to 1$^1/_2$ minutes, stirring after 1 minute or until chips are melted and mixture is smooth when stirred. Stir in $^1/_2$ teaspoon vanilla; spread evenly into prepared pan.

3. Place remaining sweetened condensed milk and chocolate chips in another small microwave-safe bowl; repeat above microwave procedure. Stir in remaining $^1/_2$ teaspoon vanilla; spread evenly over peanut butter layer.

4. Cover; refrigerate until firm. Remove from pan; place on cutting board. Peel off foil. Cut into squares. Store tightly covered in refrigerator.

NOTE: For best results, do not double this recipe.

Prep Time: 15 minutes
Cook Time: 3 minutes
Chill Time: 2 hours

Creamy Double Decker Fudge

½ cup (1 stick) butter or
   margarine

2 tablespoons sugar

1 tablespoon HERSHEY'S
   Cocoa *or* HERSHEY'S
   Dutch Processed Cocoa

½ teaspoon ground cinnamon

3 cups bite-size crisp rice
   squares cereal

3 cups bite-size crisp wheat
   squares cereal

2 cups toasted oat cereal rings

1 cup cashews

1½ cups (6-ounce package)
   dried fruit bits

1 cup HERSHEY'S Semi-Sweet
   Chocolate Chips

CHOCOLATE & FRUIT SNACK MIX

Makes about 11 cups mix

1. Place butter in 4-quart microwave-safe bowl. Microwave at HIGH (100%) 1 minute or until melted; stir in sugar, cocoa and cinnamon. Add cereals and cashews; stir until evenly coated. Microwave at HIGH 3 minutes, stirring after each minute; stir in dried fruit. Microwave at HIGH 3 minutes, stirring after each minute.

2. Cool completely; stir in chocolate chips. Store in tightly covered container in cool, dry place.

¾ cup (1½ sticks) butter (no substitutes)

1 cup REESE'S Peanut Butter Chips

½ cup HERSHEY'S Cocoa

1 can (14 ounces) sweetened condensed milk (not evaporated milk)

1 tablespoon vanilla extract

HERSHEY'S Cocoa *or* finely chopped nuts *or* graham cracker crumbs

CHOCOLATE & PEANUT BUTTER TRUFFLES

Makes about 3½ dozen candies

1. Melt butter and peanut butter chips in saucepan over very low heat. Add cocoa; stir until smooth. Add sweetened condensed milk; stir constantly until mixture is thick and glossy, about 4 minutes. Remove from heat; stir in vanilla.

2. Refrigerate 2 hours or until firm enough to handle. Shape into 1-inch balls; roll in cocoa. Refrigerate until firm, about 1 hour. Store, covered, in refrigerator.

Prep Time: 30 minutes
Cook Time: 7 minutes
Chill Time: 3 hours

HERSHEY'S HINT

Sweetened condensed milk is a canned product that is the result of evaporating about half the water from whole milk and adding cane sugar or corn syrup to sweeten and preserve the milk. The thick milk is used for desserts and candy. It should not be confused with evaporated milk.

1⅔ cups (10-ounce package) REESE'S Peanut Butter Chips

1 tablespoon shortening (do not use butter, margarine, spread or oil)

1½ cups (3-ounce can) chow mein noodles

REESE'S HAYSTACKS

Makes about 2 dozen treats

1. Line tray with wax paper.

2. Place peanut butter chips and shortening in medium microwave-safe bowl. Microwave at HIGH (100%) 1 minute; stir. If necessary, microwave at HIGH an additional 15 seconds at a time, stirring after each heating, just until chips are melted and mixture is smooth when stirred. Immediately add chow mein noodles; stir to coat.

3. Drop mixture by heaping teaspoons onto prepared tray or into paper candy cups. Let stand until firm. If necessary, cover and refrigerate several minutes until firm. Store in tightly covered container.

299

Reese's Haystacks

3 cups toasted oat cereal rings

3 cups bite-size crispy wheat
squares cereal

2 cups salted peanuts

2 cups miniature pretzels or
thin pretzel sticks

1 cup raisins

½ cup (1 stick) butter or
margarine, melted

¼ cup sugar

2 to 4 tablespoons
HERSHEY'S Cocoa

COCOA PARTY MIX

Makes about 10 cups snack mix

1. Heat oven to 250°F.

2. Combine cereals, peanuts, pretzels and raisins in large bowl. Combine melted butter, sugar and cocoa; stir into cereal mixture. Toss until ingredients are well coated. Pour mixture into 13×9×2-inch baking pan.

3. Bake 1 hour, stirring every 15 minutes. Cool completely. Store in airtight container.

MICROWAVE INSTRUCTIONS: Place butter in 4-quart microwave-safe bowl. Microwave at HIGH (100%) 1 minute or until melted; stir in sugar and cocoa. Add cereals, peanuts and pretzels; stir until well coated. Microwave at HIGH 3 minutes, stirring every minute; stir in raisins. Microwave at HIGH 3 additional minutes, stirring every minute. Cool completely. Store in airtight container. Makes about 10 cups snack mix.

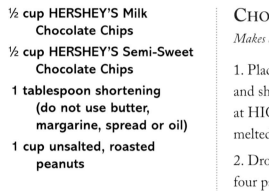

½ cup HERSHEY'S Milk
Chocolate Chips

½ cup HERSHEY'S Semi-Sweet
Chocolate Chips

1 tablespoon shortening
(do not use butter,
margarine, spread or oil)

1 cup unsalted, roasted
peanuts

CHOCOLATE PEANUT CLUSTERS

Makes about 2 dozen candies

1. Place milk chocolate chips, semi-sweet chocolate chips and shortening in small microwave-safe bowl. Microwave at HIGH (100%) 1 to $1^{1}/_{2}$ minutes or just until chips are melted and mixture is smooth when stirred. Stir in peanuts.

2. Drop by teaspoons into 1-inch-diameter candy or petit four papers. Allow to set until firm. Store in airtight container in cool, dry place.

Prep Time: 15 minutes
Cook Time: 1 minute
Cool Time: 1 hour

HERSHEY'S HINT

Shelled nuts are available year-round. They are sold in bulk, in vacuum-packed cans and jars, and in cellophane bags. Depending on the specific type of nut, they may be sold oil- or dry-roasted and salted or unsalted. Unshelled nuts are available in bulk, especially during November and December.

3 cups (1½ packages,
    12 ounces each)
    HERSHEY'S Semi-Sweet
    Chocolate Chips
1 can (14 ounces) sweetened
    condensed milk (not
    evaporated milk)
    Dash salt
1 cup chopped walnuts
1½ teaspoons vanilla extract

FOOLPROOF DARK CHOCOLATE FUDGE

Makes about 5 dozen pieces or 2 pounds

1. Line 8- or 9-inch square pan with foil, extending foil over edges of pan.

2. Melt chocolate chips with sweetened condensed milk and salt in heavy saucepan over low heat. Remove from heat; stir in walnuts and vanilla. Spread evenly into prepared pan.

3. Refrigerate 2 hours or until firm. Remove from pan; place on cutting board. Peel off foil; cut into squares. Store loosely covered at room temperature.

NOTE: For best results, do not double this recipe.

Prep Time: 10 minutes
Cook Time: 15 minutes
Chill Time: 2 hours

Foolproof Dark Chocolate Fudge

1 cup HERSHEY'S Cocoa

½ cup sugar

2 cans (14 ounces each) sweetened condensed milk (not evaporated milk)

1 cup (2 sticks) butter or margarine

1 cup coarsely chopped walnuts or pecans

1½ teaspoons vanilla extract

DEEP DARK CHOCOLATE FUDGE

Makes about 2¹/₂ pounds

1. Line 9-inch square baking pan with foil, extending foil over edges of pan.

2. Stir together cocoa and sugar in 3-quart saucepan; stir in sweetened condensed milk. Add butter; cook over medium heat, stirring constantly, until mixture boils and becomes very thick. Cook and boil over low heat 10 minutes, stirring frequently; remove from heat. Stir in nuts and vanilla; spread mixture into prepared pan.

3. Refrigerate 4 hours or until firm. Using foil, remove from pan; cut into 1-inch squares. Cover; store in refrigerator.

NOTE: For best results, do not double this recipe.

10 cups popped popcorn

1 cup whole almonds

1¾ cups (10-ounce package)
SKOR English Toffee Bits

⅔ cup light corn syrup

TOFFEE POPCORN CRUNCH

Makes about 1½ pounds popcorn

1. Heat oven to 275°F. Grease large roasting pan (or two 13×9×2-inch baking pans).

2. Place popcorn and almonds in prepared pan. Combine toffee bits and corn syrup in heavy medium saucepan. Cook over medium heat, stirring constantly, until toffee is melted (about 12 minutes). Pour over popcorn mixture; stir until evenly coated.

3. Bake 30 minutes, stirring frequently. Remove from oven; stir every 2 minutes until slightly cooled. Cool completely. Store in tightly covered container in cool, dry place.

NOTE: For best results, do not double this recipe.

1 tablespoon HERSHEY'S
  Dutch Processed Cocoa

1 ½ teaspoons sugar

1 ½ teaspoons powdered instant
  coffee

¾ cup milk

½ cup vanilla ice cream

¼ teaspoon almond extract

½ cup whipping cream

1 tablespoon butter or
  margarine

4 bars (1 ounce each)
  HERSHEY'S Semi-Sweet
  Baking Chocolate, broken
  into pieces

1 HERSHEY'S Milk Chocolate
  Bar (7 ounces), broken
  into pieces

1 tablespoon amaretto
  (almond-flavored liqueur)
  or ¼ to ½ teaspoon
  almond extract

Ground almonds

ALMOND CAPPUCCINO

Makes 1 serving

Combine cocoa, sugar and instant coffee in small saucepan; stir in milk. Add ice cream; heat to serving temperature. Do not boil. Stir in almond extract. Serve immediately. If desired, mixture may be placed in blender. Cover; blend until frothy.

ORANGE CAPPUCCINO: Omit almond extract; add ¼ teaspoon orange extract and ¼ teaspoon vanilla extract.

DOUBLE CHOCOLATE TRUFFLES

Makes about 2 dozen candies

1. Combine whipping cream and butter in small saucepan. Cook over medium heat, stirring constantly, just until mixture is very hot. Do not boil. Remove from heat; add chocolate, chocolate bar pieces and liqueur. Stir with whisk until smooth.

2. Press plastic wrap directly onto surface; cool several hours or until mixture is firm enough to handle. Shape into 1-inch balls; roll in almonds to coat. Refrigerate until firm, about 2 hours. Store in tightly covered container in refrigerator.

Double Chocolate Truffles

½ cup sugar

¼ cup HERSHEY'S Cocoa

Dash salt

⅓ cup hot water

4 cups (1 quart) milk

¾ teaspoon vanilla extract

Miniature marshmallows or
   sweetened whipped cream
   (optional)

HOT COCOA

Makes five 8-ounce servings

1. Stir together sugar, cocoa and salt in medium saucepan; stir in water. Cook over medium heat, stirring constantly, until mixture comes to a boil. Boil 2 minutes, stirring constantly. Add milk; heat to serving temperature, stirring constantly. Do not boil.

2. Remove from heat; add vanilla. Beat with rotary beater or whisk until foamy. Serve topped with marshmallows or sweetened whipped cream, if desired.

SPICED COCOA: Add ⅛ teaspoon ground cinnamon and ⅛ teaspoon ground nutmeg with vanilla. Serve with cinnamon stick, if desired.

MINT COCOA: Add ½ teaspoon mint extract or 3 tablespoons crushed hard peppermint candy or 2 to 3 tablespoons white creme de menthe with vanilla. Serve with peppermint candy stick, if desired.

CITRUS COCOA: Add ½ teaspoon orange extract or 2 to 3 tablespoons orange liqueur with vanilla.

SWISS MOCHA: Add 2 to $2^{1}/_{2}$ teaspoons powdered instant coffee with vanilla.

CANADIAN COCOA: Add $^{1}/_{2}$ teaspoon maple extract with vanilla.

COCOA AU LAIT: Omit marshmallows or sweetened whipped cream. Spoon 2 tablespoons softened vanilla ice cream on top of each cup of cocoa at serving time.

SLIM-TRIM COCOA: Omit sugar. Substitute nonfat milk for milk. Proceed as above. Stir in sugar substitute with sweetening equivalence of $^{1}/_{2}$ cup sugar with vanilla.

QUICK MICROWAVE COCOA: To make one serving, in microwave-safe cup or mug, combine 1 heaping teaspoon HERSHEY'S Cocoa, 2 heaping teaspoons sugar and dash of salt. Add 2 teaspoons cold milk; stir until smooth. Fill cup with milk. Microwave at HIGH (100%) 1 to $1^{1}/_{2}$ minutes or until hot. Stir to blend.

¼ cup HERSHEY'S Cocoa

2 tablespoons sugar

3 tablespoons warm water

1 banana, peeled and sliced

1½ cups nonfat milk

2 cups nonfat frozen yogurt

2 bars (1 ounce each) HERSHEY'S Unsweetened Baking Chocolate, broken into pieces

1 can (14 ounces) sweetened condensed milk (not evaporated milk)

4 cups boiling water

1 teaspoon vanilla extract

Dash salt

Whipped cream (optional)

Ground cinnamon (optional)

LUSCIOUS COCOA SMOOTHIES

Makes 4 servings

Stir together cocoa and sugar in small bowl. Add water; stir until well blended. In blender, place banana and cocoa mixture. Cover; blend until smooth. Add milk and frozen yogurt. Cover; blend until smooth. Serve immediately.

ROYAL HOT CHOCOLATE

Makes 8 servings

Melt chocolate in large heavy saucepan over low heat. Stir in sweetened condensed milk. Gradually add water, stirring until well blended. Stir in vanilla and salt. Garnish with whipped cream and cinnamon, if desired. Serve immediately.

Left to right: Royal Hot Chocolate, Mocha Shake (page 312), Luscious Cocoa Smoothie

3 large ripe bananas

9 wooden popsicle sticks

2 cups (12-ounce package) HERSHEY'S Semi-Sweet Chocolate Chips

2 tablespoons shortening (do not use butter, margarine, spread or oil)

1½ cups coarsely chopped unsalted, roasted peanuts

CHOCOLATE-COVERED BANANA POPS
Makes 9 pops

1. Peel bananas; cut each into thirds. Insert a wooden stick into each banana piece; place on wax paper-covered tray. Cover; freeze until firm.

2. Place chocolate chips and shortening in microwave-safe container. Microwave at HIGH (100%) 1½ to 2 minutes or until chocolate is melted and mixture is smooth when stirred. Remove bananas from freezer just before dipping. Dip each piece into warm chocolate, covering completely; allow excess to drip off. Immediately roll in peanuts. Cover; return to freezer. Serve frozen.

VARIATION: HERSHEY'S Milk Chocolate Chips or HERSHEY'S MINI CHIPS Semi-Sweet Chocolate may be substituted for Semi-Sweet Chocolate Chips.

¼ cup warm water

2 tablespoons HERSHEY'S Cocoa

1 tablespoon sugar

1 to 2 teaspoons powdered instant coffee

½ cup milk

2 cups vanilla ice cream

MOCHA SHAKE
Makes 3 servings

Place water, cocoa, sugar and instant coffee in blender container. Cover; blend briefly on low speed. Add milk. Cover; blend well on high speed. Add ice cream. Cover; blend until smooth. Serve immediately. Garnish as desired.

1 tablespoon sugar

2 teaspoons HERSHEY'S Cocoa

1 tablespoon hot water

1 scoop vanilla ice cream

   Cold root beer

1 cup cold milk or half-and-half

½ cup mashed ripe banana
   (about 1 medium)

½ cup creme de banana
   liqueur (banana-flavored
   liqueur)

⅓ cup HERSHEY'S Syrup

2½ cups ice cubes

CHOCOLATE ROOT BEER FLOAT

Makes one 12-ounce serving

1. Stir together sugar and cocoa in 12-ounce glass; stir in water.

2. Add ice cream and enough root beer to half fill glass; stir gently. Fill glass with root beer; stir. Serve immediately.

FROZEN BANANA SMOOTHIE

Makes about three 9-ounce servings

1. Place all ingredients in blender container. Cover; blend on high speed 2 minutes.

2. Reduce speed; blend 1 minute longer or until frothy. Serve immediately.

¾ cup cold milk

¼ cup sliced fresh strawberries

2 tablespoons HERSHEY'S Syrup

2 tablespoons plus 2 small scoops vanilla ice cream, divided

Cold ginger ale or club soda

Fresh strawberry

Mint leaves (optional)

CHOCO-BERRY COOLER

Makes one 14-ounce serving

1. Place milk, strawberries, chocolate syrup and 2 tablespoons ice cream in blender container. Cover and blend until smooth.

2. Alternate remaining 2 scoops of ice cream and chocolate mixture in tall ice cream soda glass; fill glass with ginger ale. Garnish with a fresh strawberry and mint leaves, if desired. Serve immediately.

VARIATIONS: Before blending, substitute one of the following fruits for fresh strawberries: 3 tablespoons frozen strawberries with syrup, thawed; $1/2$ of peeled fresh peach or $1/3$ cup canned peach slices; 2 slices canned pineapple or $1/4$ cup canned crushed pineapple; $1/4$ cup sweetened fresh raspberries or 3 tablespoons frozen raspberries with syrup, thawed.

Top to bottom: Choco-Berry Cooler, Chocolate Root Beer Float (page 313), Frozen Banana Smoothie (page 313)

8 tablespoons (1 stick) butter or margarine, divided

¾ cup packed light brown sugar

4 tablespoons HERSHEY'S Cocoa, divided

5 teaspoons water

1 teaspoon vanilla extract

½ cup coarsely chopped nuts (optional)

2 cans (8 ounces each) refrigerated quick crescent dinner rolls

2 tablespoons granulated sugar

CHOCOLATE QUICKIE STICKIES

Makes 4 dozen small rolls

1. Heat oven to 350°F.

2. Melt 6 tablespoons butter in small saucepan over low heat; add brown sugar, 3 tablespoons cocoa and water. Cook over medium heat, stirring constantly, just until mixture comes to boil. Remove from heat; stir in vanilla. Spoon about 1 teaspoon chocolate mixture into each of 48 small muffin cups (1³/₄ inches in diameter). Sprinkle ¹/₂ teaspoon nuts, if desired, into each cup; set aside.

3. Unroll dough; separate into 8 rectangles; firmly press perforations to seal. Melt remaining 2 tablespoons butter; brush over rectangles. Stir together granulated sugar and remaining 1 tablespoon cocoa; sprinkle over rectangles. Starting at longer side, roll up each rectangle; pinch seams to seal. Cut each roll into 6 equal pieces. Press gently into prepared pans, cut sides down.

4. Bake 11 to 13 minutes or until light brown. Remove from oven; let cool 30 seconds. Invert onto cookie sheet. Let stand 1 minute; remove pans. Serve warm or cool completely.

NOTE: Rolls can be baked in two 8-inch round baking pans. Heat oven to 350°F. Cook chocolate mixture as directed; spread half of mixture in each pan. Prepare rolls as directed; place 24 pieces, cut sides down, in each pan. Bake 20 to 22 minutes. Cool and remove pans as directed above.

317

Chocolate Quickie Stickies

2¼ cups all-purpose flour

½ cup HERSHEY'S Cocoa

2½ teaspoons baking powder

½ teaspoon baking soda

¼ teaspoon ground cinnamon

¼ teaspoon ground mace

¼ teaspoon salt

¾ cup granulated sugar

1½ tablespoons butter, softened

1 egg

½ cup milk

¼ cup powdered sugar

Dash ground cinnamon

SPICED COCOA DOUGHNUTS

Makes about 2 dozen doughnuts

1. Stir together flour, cocoa, baking powder, baking soda, ¼ teaspoon cinnamon, mace and salt in medium bowl. Beat sugar and butter in large bowl until creamy. Add egg; beat well. Add flour mixture alternately with milk, mixing until well blended; shape into ball.

2. On lightly floured surface, roll dough to ¼-inch thickness. With floured 2½-inch doughnut cutter, cut into rings. Reroll dough as necessary. Fry two or three doughnuts at a time in deep hot fat (375°F) about 30 seconds, turning once with slotted spoon. Drain on paper towels. Repeat with remaining doughnuts.

3. Stir together powdered sugar and dash cinnamon; sprinkle over tops of warm doughnuts.

½ cup granulated sugar

½ cup packed light brown sugar

2 to 3 tablespoons powdered instant coffee

2 teaspoons vanilla extract

1¾ cups all-purpose flour

1 tablespoon baking powder

½ teaspoon salt

2 eggs

⅔ cup milk

1½ cups coarsely chopped walnuts

¾ cup HERSHEY'S Semi-Sweet Chocolate Chips

COFFEE WALNUT CHOCOLATE CHIP MUFFINS

Makes 12 muffins

1. Heat oven to 350°F. Line twelve muffin cups (2½ inches in diameter) with paper bake cups.

2. Beat butter, granulated sugar, brown sugar, coffee and vanilla in large bowl until creamy. Stir together flour, baking powder and salt. Beat together eggs and milk; add alternately with flour mixture to butter mixture, stirring just to combine. Stir in walnuts and chocolate chips. Fill muffin cups ½ full with batter.

3. Bake 20 to 25 minutes. Cool 5 minutes; remove from pans to wire rack. Cool completely.

HOLIDAY FAVORITES

1 cup (2 sticks) butter or margarine, divided

1½ cups finely crushed unsalted thin pretzels or pretzel sticks

1 cup HERSHEY'S MINI KISSES Milk Chocolate *or* Semi-Sweet Baking Pieces

1 can (14 ounces) sweetened condensed milk (not evaporated milk)

¾ cup HERSHEY'S Cocoa

2 cups MOUNDS Sweetened Coconut Flakes, tinted*

To tint coconut: Place 1 teaspoon water and ½ teaspoon red food color in small bowl; stir in 2 cups coconut flakes. With fork, toss until evenly tinted.

SWEETHEART LAYER BARS

Makes about 36 bars

1. Heat oven to 350°F.

2. Put ¾ cup butter in 13×9×2-inch baking pan; place in oven just until butter melts. Remove from oven. Stir in crushed pretzels; press evenly onto bottom of pan. Sprinkle Mini Kisses over pretzel layer.

3. Place sweetened condensed milk, cocoa and remaining ¼ cup butter in small microwave-safe bowl. Microwave at HIGH (100%) 1 to 1½ minutes or until mixture is melted and smooth when stirred; carefully pour over pretzel layer in pan. Top with coconut; press firmly down onto chocolate layer.

4. Bake 25 to 30 minutes or until lightly browned around edges. Cool completely in pan on wire rack. Cut into heart-shaped pieces with cookie cutters or cut into bars.

Sweetheart Layer Bars

⅔ cup butter or margarine, softened

1¾ cups sugar

2 eggs

1 teaspoon vanilla extract

1¾ cups all-purpose flour

¾ cup HERSHEY'S Cocoa *or* HERSHEY'S Dutch Processed Cocoa

1½ teaspoons baking soda

1 teaspoon salt

1½ cups dairy sour cream

Pink Buttercream Frosting (page 324)

Maraschino cherries (optional)

FUDGEY VALENTINE CAKE

Makes 10 to 12 servings

1. Heat oven to 350°F. Grease and flour two 9-inch heart-shaped pans.*

2. Beat butter and sugar until creamy in large bowl. Add eggs and vanilla; beat well. Stir together flour, cocoa, baking soda and salt; add to butter mixture alternately with sour cream, beating well after each addition. Beat 3 minutes on medium speed of mixer. Pour batter evenly into prepared pans.

3. Bake 35 to 40 minutes or until wooden pick inserted in centers comes out clean. Cool 10 minutes; remove from pans to wire racks. Cool completely. Prepare Pink Buttercream Frosting; spread between layers and over top and sides of cake. Garnish with cherries, if desired.

One 8-inch square baking pan and one 8-inch round baking pan (each must be 2 inches deep) may be substituted for heart-shaped pans. Prepare, bake and cool cake as directed above. Cut round layer in half, forming two half circles; place cut edge of each half circle against sides of square layer to form heart.

continued on page 324

Clockwise from top: Fudgey Valentine Cake, Chocolate and White Hearts (page 325), Cocoa Cookie Hearts (page 326)

Genuine CHOCOLATE Flavor

Fudgey Valentine Cake, continued

Pink Buttercream Frosting
- ½ **cup (1 stick) butter or margarine, softened**
- 4¼ **cups powdered sugar**
- 4 **tablespoons milk**
- 2 **teaspoons vanilla extract**
- ¼ **teaspoon red food color**

Beat butter in small bowl until creamy. Gradually add powdered sugar alternately with combined milk and vanilla, beating well after each addition until smooth and of spreading consistency. Stir in food color. Add additional milk, 1 teaspoon at a time, if needed.

Hershey's Hint

Oven temperatures can vary significantly depending on the oven model and manufacturer, so watch your dessert carefully and check for doneness using the test given in the recipe.

1 cup HERSHEY'S Semi-Sweet
Chocolate Chips *or*
HERSHEY'S Milk Chocolate
Chips

2 tablespoons shortening (do
not use butter, margarine,
spread or oil), divided

¾ cup HERSHEY'S Premier
White Chips

¼ cup finely ground nuts

CHOCOLATE & WHITE HEARTS

Makes about 10 candies

1. Place chocolate chips and 1 tablespoon shortening in small microwave-safe bowl. Microwave at HIGH (100%) 1 minute; stir. If necessary, microwave at HIGH an additional 30 seconds at a time, stirring after each heating, just until chips are melted when stirred.

2. Spoon into heart-shaped ice cube tray or candy molds, filling each $^1/_2$ full; tap molds to release air bubbles and smooth surface. Refrigerate 8 to 10 minutes to partially set chocolate.

3. Meanwhile, place white chips and 1 tablespoon shortening in small microwave-safe bowl. Microwave at HIGH 1 minute; stir. If necessary, microwave at HIGH an additional 30 seconds, stirring after each heating, just until chips are melted when stirred; stir in nuts.

4. Spoon over chocolate layer; tap to smooth surface. Refrigerate several hours or until firm. Invert tray or molds; tap lightly to release candies.

ALMOND HEARTS: Add 2 or 3 drops almond extract to melted chocolate chips.

CHERRY HEARTS: Omit nuts; add $^1/_4$ cup finely chopped red candied cherries and 2 or 3 drops red food color to melted white chips.

MINT HEARTS: Add $^1/_4$ teaspoon mint extract and 2 or 3 drops red or green food color to melted white chips.

½ cup (1 stick) butter or
    margarine, softened

1 cup sugar

2 eggs

2 cups all-purpose flour

½ cup HERSHEY'S Cocoa

1 teaspoon baking powder

½ teaspoon baking soda

½ teaspoon salt

    Valentine Frosting (recipe
    follows)

COCOA COOKIE HEARTS

Makes about 4 dozen cookies

1. Beat butter, sugar and eggs in large bowl until fluffy. Stir together flour, cocoa, baking powder, baking soda and salt; gradually add to butter mixture, beating until blended. Cover; refrigerate dough until firm enough to handle.

2. Heat oven to 350°F.

3. On lightly floured surface, roll dough to ⅛-inch thickness; cut with heart-shaped cookie cutter. Place on ungreased cookie sheet. Bake 5 to 7 minutes or until no imprint remains when cookies are touched lightly in center. Cool 1 minute; remove from cookie sheet to wire racks. Cool completely.

4. Prepare Valentine Frosting; spread onto cookies. Decorate as desired.

VALENTINE FROSTING

- 1 ½ **cups powdered sugar**
- 2 **tablespoons butter, margarine or shortening**
- 2 **tablespoons milk**
- ½ **teaspoon vanilla extract**

Beat powdered sugar, butter, milk and vanilla in small bowl until smooth and of spreading consistency. Add additional milk, 1 teaspoon at a time, if needed.

PINK VALENTINE FROSTING: Stir in 2 to 3 drops red food color, tinting as desired.

CHOCOLATE VALENTINE FROSTING: Stir 3 tablespoons HERSHEY'S Cocoa into powdered sugar. Proceed as directed above, increasing milk to 3 tablespoons.

HERSHEY'S HINT

Food colorings are edible dyes—usually red, green, blue and yellow—used to tint frostings and candies. The most popular are liquid colors available at supermarkets. They impart intense color and should initially be used sparingly, a drop or two at a time.

½ cup sliced almonds, toasted*

7 eggs, separated

1 ¼ cups sugar, divided

1 tablespoon water

¼ teaspoon freshly grated orange peel

⅓ cup potato starch

¼ cup matzo cake meal

⅓ cup HERSHEY'S Cocoa

¼ teaspoon salt

Whole blanched almonds and strips of orange peel (optional garnish)

Cocoa-Orange Sauce (recipe follows, optional)

To toast almonds: Heat oven to 350°F. Place almonds in single layer in shallow baking pan. Bake 7 to 8 minutes, stirring occasionally, until light brown. Cool completely.

PASSOVER CHOCOLATE ALMOND-ORANGE CAKE

Makes 12 to 16 servings

1. Heat oven to 300°F. Place toasted almonds in bowl of food processor; process until ground. Set aside.

2. Beat egg yolks in large bowl until lemon-colored. Gradually add 1 cup sugar, beating until thick. Stir in water and orange peel. Stir together potato starch, cake meal and cocoa; fold into yolk mixture. Fold in ground almonds.

3. Beat egg whites and salt in separate large bowl until foamy. Gradually add remaining ¼ cup sugar in small amounts, beating until stiff peaks form. Gently fold about 1 cup egg white mixture into yolk mixture; fold all yolk mixture into remaining whites. Pour into ungreased 10-inch tube pan.

4. Bake 30 minutes. Without opening oven door, *increase oven temperature to 325°F.* Bake 15 minutes or until top springs back when touched lightly. Invert cake on heat-proof funnel or bottle. Cool completely. Carefully run knife along side of pan to loosen cake; remove from pan. Garnish as desired. Serve with Cocoa-Orange Sauce, if desired.

COCOA-ORANGE SAUCE: Combine 1 cup sugar and ½ cup HERSHEY'S Cocoa in saucepan. Add ⅔ cup water. Cook over medium heat, stirring constantly, until mixture comes to full boil; boil, stirring occasionally, about 5 minutes. Add ¾ teaspoon freshly grated orange peel; cook 1 minute. Cool to room temperature.

329

Passover Chocolate Almond-Orange Cake

1 cup sliced or slivered
   almonds, toasted*

1 cup plus 1 tablespoon sugar,
   divided

¾ cup (1½ sticks) butter

½ cup HERSHEY'S Cocoa

5 eggs, separated

⅛ teaspoon salt

Warm Chocolate Sauce
   (recipe follows)

*To toast almonds: Heat oven to 350°F.
Place almonds in single layer in shallow
baking pan. Bake 7 to 8 minutes, stirring
occasionally, until light brown. Cool
completely.*

330

CHOCOLATE PASSOVER TORTE

Makes about 12 servings

1. Heat oven to 375°F. Grease bottom of 9-inch springform pan; line bottom with foil.

2. Place toasted almonds in bowl of food processor with 1 tablespoon sugar; process until finely ground.

3. Melt butter in small saucepan; cool slightly. Stir in cocoa; cool.

4. Beat egg yolks with ¾ cup sugar in large bowl until pale yellow. Add chocolate mixture and salt; mix well. Stir in almonds.

5. Beat egg whites until foamy. Gradually add remaining ¼ cup sugar, beating until stiff but not dry. Add about one-fourth beaten egg whites to chocolate mixture; stir until well blended. Gradually fold remaining egg whites into chocolate. Pour into prepared pan.

6. Bake 40 to 45 minutes or until set. Cool 10 minutes in pan on wire rack. Unmold and carefully peel off foil. Cool completely. Serve with Warm Chocolate Sauce.

WARM CHOCOLATE SAUCE

Makes about 1¹/₃ cups sauce

- ⅓ cup packed light brown sugar
- 2 tablespoons HERSHEY'S Cocoa
- 1 teaspoon potato starch
- ¾ cup evaporated milk
- ¼ cup (½ stick) butter

Stir together sugar, cocoa and potato starch in small saucepan. Gradually stir in evaporated milk. Cook over medium heat, stirring constantly, until mixture thickens. Add butter; stir until melted. Cool slightly.

HERSHEY'S HINT

Use clear glass measuring cups with calibrations marked on their sides when measuring liquid ingredients. An ideal set of liquid measures includes 1-cup, 2-cup and 4-cup measures. Small amounts of liquid (under ¼ cup) can be measured with measuring spoons by filling the spoon to the rim.

2 cups sugar

1¾ cups all-purpose flour

¾ cup HERSHEY'S Cocoa *or* HERSHEY'S Dutch Processed Cocoa

1½ teaspoons baking powder

1½ teaspoons baking soda

1 teaspoon salt

2 eggs

1 cup milk

½ cup vegetable oil

2 teaspoons vanilla extract

1 cup boiling water

Creamy Vanilla Frosting (recipe follows)

Green, red and yellow food color

3¾ cups (10-ounce package) MOUNDS Sweetened Coconut Flakes, divided and tinted*

Suggested garnishes (marshmallows, HERSHEY'S MINI KISSES Milk Chocolate Baking Pieces, licorice, jelly beans)

*To tint coconut, combine ¾ teaspoon water with several drops green food color in small bowl. Stir in 1¼ cups coconut. Toss with fork until evenly tinted. Repeat with red and yellow food colors and remaining coconut.

EASTER BASKETS AND BUNNIES CUPCAKES

Makes about 33 cupcakes

1. Heat oven to 350°F. Line muffin cups (2½ inches in diameter) with paper bake cups.

2. Stir together sugar, flour, cocoa, baking powder, baking soda and salt in large bowl. Add eggs, milk, oil and vanilla; beat on medium speed of mixer 2 minutes. Stir in boiling water (batter will be thin). Fill muffin cups ⅔ full with batter.

3. Bake 22 to 25 minutes or until wooden pick inserted in centers comes out clean. Cool completely. Prepare Creamy Vanilla Frosting; frost cupcakes. Immediately press desired color tinted coconut onto each cupcake. Garnish as desired to resemble Easter basket or bunny.

CREAMY VANILLA FROSTING: Beat ⅓ cup softened butter or margarine in medium bowl. Add 1 cup powdered sugar and 1½ teaspoons vanilla extract; beat well. Add 2½ cups powdered sugar alternately with ¼ cup milk, beating to spreading consistency. Makes about 2 cups frosting.

333

Easter Baskets and Bunnies Cupcakes

2 cups sugar

1¾ cups all-purpose flour

¾ cup HERSHEY'S Cocoa

2 teaspoons baking soda

1 teaspoon baking powder

1 teaspoon salt

2 eggs

1 cup buttermilk or sour milk*

1 cup boiling water

½ cup vegetable oil

1 teaspoon vanilla extract

Vanilla Frosting (recipe follows)

Chocolate stars or blue and red decorating icing (in tube)

To sour milk: Use 1 tablespoon white vinegar plus milk to equal 1 cup.

PATRIOTIC COCOA CUPCAKES

Makes about 30 cupcakes

1. Heat oven to 350°F. Grease and flour muffin cups (2½-inches in diameter) or line with paper bake cups.

2. Combine dry ingredients in large bowl. Add eggs, buttermilk, water, oil and vanilla; beat on medium speed of mixer 2 minutes (batter will be thin). Fill cups ⅔ full with batter.

3. Bake 15 minutes or until wooden pick inserted in centers comes out clean. Remove cupcakes from pan. Cool completely. To make chocolate stars for garnish, if desired, cut several cupcakes into ½-inch slices; cut out star shapes from cake slices. Frost remaining cupcakes. Garnish with chocolate stars or with blue and red decorating icing.

VANILLA FROSTING: Beat ¼ cup (½ stick) softened butter, ¼ cup shortening and 2 teaspoons vanilla extract. Add 1 cup powdered sugar; beat until creamy. Add 3 cups powdered sugar alternately with 3 to 4 tablespoons milk, beating to spreading consistency. Makes about 2⅓ cups frosting.

Patriotic Cocoa Cupcakes

1⅔ cups all-purpose flour

1½ cups sugar

½ cup HERSHEY'S Cocoa

1½ teaspoons baking soda

1 teaspoon salt

½ teaspoon baking powder

2 eggs

1½ cups buttermilk or sour milk*

½ cup shortening (do not use butter, margarine, spread or oil)

1 teaspoon vanilla extract

One-Bowl Buttercream Frosting (page 338)

Spider Web (page 338)

*To sour milk: Use 4½ teaspoons white vinegar plus milk to equal 1½ cups.

CHOCOLATE SPIDER WEB CAKE

Makes 12 servings

1. Heat oven to 350°F. Thoroughly grease and flour two 9-inch round baking pans.

2. Combine dry ingredients in large bowl; add eggs, buttermilk, shortening and vanilla. Beat on low speed of mixer 1 minute, scraping bowl constantly. Beat on high speed 3 minutes, scraping bowl occasionally. Pour batter into prepared pans.

3. Bake 30 to 35 minutes or until wooden pick inserted in center comes out clean. Cool 10 minutes; remove from pans to wire racks. Cool completely.

4. Frost with One-Bowl Buttercream Frosting. Immediately pipe or drizzle Spider Web in 4 or 5 circles on top of cake. Using a knife or wooden pick, immediately draw 8 to 10 lines from center to edges of cake at regular intervals to form web. Garnish with "spider," using cookie, licorice and other candies. *continued on page 338*

Chocolate Spider Web Cake

Chocolate Spider Web Cake, continued

ONE-BOWL BUTTERCREAM FROSTING
Makes about 2 cups frosting

    6 tablespoons butter or margarine, softened
2⅔ cups powdered sugar
    ½ cup HERSHEY'S Cocoa
    4 to 6 tablespoons milk
    1 teaspoon vanilla extract

Beat butter; add powdered sugar and cocoa alternately with milk, beating to spreading consistency. Stir in vanilla.

SPIDER WEB: Place ¹/₂ cup HERSHEY'S Premier White Chips and ¹/₂ teaspoon shortening (do not use butter, margarine, spread or oil) in small heavy seal-top plastic bag. Microwave at HIGH (100%) 45 seconds. Squeeze gently. If necessary, microwave an additional 10 to 15 seconds; squeeze until chips are melted. With scissors, make small diagonal cut in bottom corner of bag; squeeze mixture onto cake as directed.

5 cups crisp rice cereal

6 tablespoons butter or
   margarine

3 cups miniature
   marshmallows or 30 large
   marshmallows

1⅔ cups (10-ounce package)
   REESE'S Peanut Butter
   Chips

⅓ cup HERSHEY'S Cocoa

⅓ cup light corn syrup

BEWITCHING COCOA BITES

Makes about 3½ dozen treats

1. Measure cereal; set aside. Melt butter in large saucepan over low heat. Add marshmallows, peanut butter chips and cocoa. Cook over low heat, stirring constantly, until marshmallows and chips are melted. Remove from heat. Stir in corn syrup. Add cereal; stir until well coated.

2. Shape mixture into 1½-inch balls, stirring a few times during shaping. Place on cookie sheet. Cool completely. Store in cool, dry place.

MICROWAVE DIRECTIONS: Microwave butter, covered, in large microwave-safe bowl at HIGH (100%) 45 seconds or until melted. Add marshmallows, peanut butter chips and cocoa; stir. Microwave at HIGH 1½ minutes; stir until mixture is smooth. Stir in corn syrup. Add cereal; stir until well coated. Shape as directed above.

2/3 cup butter or margarine, softened

1 cup sugar

2 teaspoons vanilla extract

2 eggs

2½ cups all-purpose flour

½ cup HERSHEY'S Cocoa

¼ teaspoon baking soda

½ teaspoon salt

1 cup HERSHEY'S MINI CHIPS Semi-Sweet Chocolate

1 to 2 packages (10 ounces each) HERSHEY'S Premier White Chips

1 to 2 tablespoons shortening (do not use butter, margarine, spread or oil)

Additional HERSHEY'S MINI CHIPS Semi-Sweet Chocolate

YUMMY MUMMY COOKIES

Makes about 2½ dozen cookies

1. Beat butter, sugar and vanilla in large bowl until creamy. Add eggs; beat well. Stir together flour, cocoa, baking soda and salt; gradually add to butter mixture, beating until blended. Stir in 1 cup Mini Chips. Refrigerate dough 15 to 20 minutes or until firm enough to handle.

2. Heat oven to 350°F. To form mummy body, using 1 tablespoon dough, roll into 3½-inch carrot shape; place on ungreased cookie sheet. To form head, using 1 teaspoon dough, roll into ball the size and shape of a grape; press onto wide end of body. Repeat procedure with remaining dough. Bake 8 to 9 minutes or until set. Cool slightly; remove from cookie sheet to wire racks. Cool completely.

3. Place 1²/₃ cups (10-ounce package) white chips and 1 tablespoon shortening in microwave-safe pie plate or shallow bowl. Microwave at HIGH (100%) 1 minute; stir until chips are melted.

4. Coat tops of cookies by placing one cookie at a time on table knife or narrow metal spatula; spoon white chip mixture evenly over cookie to coat. (If mixture begins to thicken, return to microwave for a few seconds). Place coated cookies on wax paper. Melt additional chips with shortening, if needed, for additional coating. As coating begins to set on cookies, using a toothpick, score lines and facial features into coating to resemble mummy. Place 2 Mini Chips on each cookie for eyes. Store, covered, in cool, dry place.

341

Yummy Mummy Cookies

¼ cup (½ stick) butter or margarine

30 large marshmallows or 3 cups miniature marshmallows

¼ cup light corn syrup

½ cup REESE'S Creamy Peanut Butter

⅓ cup HERSHEY'S Semi-Sweet Chocolate Chips

4½ cups crisp rice cereal

BOO BITES

Makes about 4 dozen pieces

1. Line cookie sheet with wax paper.

2. Melt butter in large saucepan over low heat. Add marshmallows. Cook, stirring constantly, until marshmallows are melted. Remove from heat. Add corn syrup; stir until well blended. Add peanut butter and chocolate chips; stir until chips are melted and mixture is well blended.

3. Add cereal; stir until evenly coated. Cool slightly. With wet hands, shape mixture into $1^1/_2$-inch balls; place balls on prepared cookie sheet. Cool completely. Store in tightly covered container in cool, dry place.

HERSHEY'S HINT

For even baking and browning of cookies, bake them in the center of the oven. If the heat distribution in your oven is uneven, turn the cookie sheet halfway through the baking time. Most cookies bake quickly and should be watched carefully to avoid overbaking.

½ cup (1 stick) margarine

2 tablespoons sugar

2 tablespoons HERSHEY'S
  Cocoa

3 cups bite-size crisp wheat
  squares cereal

3 cups toasted oat cereal rings

2 cups miniature pretzels

1 cup salted peanuts

2 cups raisins

PARTY MIX WITH COCOA

Makes 10 cups mix

Place margarine in 4-quart microwave-safe bowl; microwave at HIGH (100%) 1 to $1^{1}/_{2}$ minutes or until melted. Stir in sugar and cocoa. Add cereals, pretzels and peanuts to margarine mixture; stir until well coated. Microwave at HIGH 3 minutes, stirring every minute. Stir in raisins. Microwave at HIGH 3 minutes, stirring every minute. Cool completely. Store in airtight container at room temperature.

¾ cup packed light brown sugar

½ cup butter flavor shortening

1 egg

1 tablespoon water

1 teaspoon vanilla extract

1 ¼ cups all-purpose flour

½ teaspoon baking soda

¼ teaspoon salt

1 cup REESE'S Peanut Butter Chips

1 cup miniature marshmallows

½ cup HERSHEY'S Semi-Sweet Chocolate Chips

½ cup chopped pecans

Chocolate Drizzle (recipe follows)

Orange Drizzle (recipe follows)

HALLOWEEN COOKIE PIZZA

Makes about 16 to 20 servings

1. Heat oven to 350°F. Lightly grease 12-inch round pizza pan.

2. Beat brown sugar and shortening in large bowl until creamy. Add egg, water and vanilla; beat well. Stir together flour, baking soda and salt; add to sugar mixture, beating on low speed of mixer until well blended. Stir in peanut butter chips. Spread batter onto prepared pan to within $1/2$ inch of edge.

3. Bake 11 to 13 minutes or until set. Remove from oven. Sprinkle marshmallows, chocolate chips and pecans over top. Return to oven. Bake 5 to 7 minutes or until marshmallows are lightly browned. Cool completely.

4. Prepare Chocolate Drizzle and Orange Drizzle. Drizzle Chocolate Drizzle over top. Drizzle Orange Drizzle over chocolate. Let stand about 1 hour until drizzles set. Cut into wedges.

CHOCOLATE DRIZZLE: In small microwave-safe bowl, place $1/4$ cup HERSHEY'S Semi-Sweet Chocolate Chips and $1^{1}/2$ teaspoons butter flavor shortening. Microwave at MEDIUM (50%) 1 minute; stir. If necessary, microwave at MEDIUM an additional 15 seconds at a time, stirring after each heating, just until chips are melted when stirred.

ORANGE DRIZZLE: In small bowl, stir together $1/2$ cup powdered sugar, 1 tablespoon water, 3 drops yellow food color and 2 drops red food color; stir until well blended.

Halloween Cookie Pizza

⅓ cup butter or margarine,
    softened

⅓ cup granulated sugar

⅓ cup packed light brown sugar

1 egg

1¼ teaspoons vanilla extract

1⅓ cups all-purpose flour

¾ teaspoon baking powder

¼ teaspoon baking soda

¼ teaspoon salt

2 tablespoons milk

1¼ cups coarsely chopped fresh
    cranberries

½ cup coarsely chopped
    walnuts

1⅔ cups HERSHEY'S Premier
    White Chips, divided

White Glaze (recipe follows)

GLAZED CRANBERRY MINI-CAKES

Makes about 3 dozen mini-cakes

1. Heat oven to 350°F. Lightly grease small muffin cups (1¾ inches in diameter) or line with paper bake cups.

2. Beat butter, granulated sugar, brown sugar, egg and vanilla in large bowl until fluffy. Stir together flour, baking powder, baking soda and salt; gradually blend into butter mixture. Add milk; stir until blended. Stir in cranberries, walnuts and ⅔ cup white chips (reserve remaining chips for glaze). Fill muffin cups ⅞ full with batter.

3. Bake 18 to 20 minutes or until wooden pick inserted in centers comes out clean. Cool 5 minutes; remove from pans to wire rack. Cool completely. Prepare White Glaze; drizzle over tops of mini-cakes. Refrigerate 10 minutes to set glaze.

WHITE GLAZE: Place remaining 1 cup HERSHEY'S Premier White Chips in small microwave-safe bowl; sprinkle 2 tablespoons vegetable oil over chips. Microwave at HIGH (100% power) 30 seconds; stir. If necessary, microwave at HIGH an additional 30 seconds or just until chips are melted when stirred.

Glazed Cranberry Mini-Cakes

Walnut-Chip Filling
(recipe follows)

2½ to 2¾ cups all-purpose flour,
divided

¼ cup sugar

½ teaspoon salt

1 package active dry yeast

½ cup dairy sour cream

¼ cup (½ stick) butter

¼ cup water

2 tablespoons milk

2 egg yolks (reserve whites
for filling)

Sugar Glaze or Two-Tone
Glaze (recipe follows)

WALNUT KUCHEN

Makes 2 loaves

1. Prepare Walnut-Chip filling. Grease cookie sheet; set aside.

2. Stir together 1 cup flour, sugar, salt and yeast in large bowl; set aside. Stir together sour cream, butter, water and milk in small saucepan. Cook over low heat, stirring occasionally, until very warm (120°F to 130°F). Gradually add sour cream mixture to flour mixture; beat on medium speed of mixer 2 minutes. Add egg yolks and ¹/₂ cup flour; beat on high speed 2 minutes. Gradually stir in enough flour to make soft dough. When dough becomes difficult to stir, turn out onto well-floured surface. Knead in enough remaining flour until dough is elastic and forms smooth ball, 3 to 5 minutes. Cover; allow to rest 15 minutes.

3. Divide dough in half. On lightly floured surface, roll each half into 12×10-inch rectangle. Spread about 1¹/₄ cups Walnut-Chip Filling onto each rectangle to within ¹/₂ inch of edges. Roll up, jelly-roll style, starting from one long side; pinch to seal edges. Place on prepared cookie sheet, sealed edge up, just slightly curving roll. Cover with towel; let rise in warm place until doubled, about 1 to 1¹/₂ hours.

4. Heat oven to 350°F.

5. Bake 20 minutes. Loosely cover with foil; bake additional 15 minutes or until golden brown. Transfer kuchen to wire rack; brush lightly with butter. Cool completely. Just before serving, drizzle Sugar Glaze or Two-Tone Glaze over top.

WALNUT-CHIP FILLING

Makes about 2¹/₂ cups filling

2 egg whites; reserved form kuchen

¹/₃ cup sugar

Dash salt

2 cups ground walnuts

1 cup HERSHEY'S MINI CHIPS Semi-Sweet Chocolate

Beat egg whites in small bowl until foamy. Gradually add sugar and salt, beating until stiff peaks form. Fold in walnuts and Mini Chips.

SUGAR GLAZE: Stir together 1¹/₂ cups powdered sugar, 2 to 3 tablespoons milk and ¹/₂ teaspoon vanilla extract in medium bowl until of drizzling consistency. Makes about ²/₃ cup glaze.

TWO-TONE GLAZE: Prepare Sugar Glaze as directed above. Pour half of glaze into small bowl; stir in 2 tablespoons HERSHEY'S Cocoa and 1 to 2 teaspoons milk until smooth.

1 cup (2 sticks) butter or
    margarine, softened

1 cup sugar

1 egg

1 teaspoon vanilla extract

1¾ cups all-purpose flour

½ cup HERSHEY'S Cocoa

1½ teaspoons baking powder

½ teaspoon salt

    Buttercream Frosting
    (recipe follows)

HANUKKAH COIN COOKIES

Makes about 4½ dozen cookies

1. Beat butter, sugar, egg and vanilla in large bowl until well blended. Stir together flour, cocoa, baking powder and salt; gradually add to butter mixture, beating until well blended. Divide dough in half; place each half on separate sheet of wax paper.

2. Shape each portion into log, about 7 inches long. Wrap each log in wax paper or plastic wrap. Refrigerate until firm, at least 8 hours.

3. Heat oven to 325°F. Cut logs into ¼-inch-thick slices. Place on ungreased cookie sheet.

4. Bake 8 to 10 minutes or until set. Cool slightly; remove from cookie sheet to wire racks. Cool completely. Prepare Buttercream Frosting; spread over tops of cookies.

BUTTERCREAM FROSTING

Makes about 1 cup frosting

    ¼ cup (½ stick) butter, softened

1½ cups powdered sugar

  1 to 2 tablespoons milk

  ½ teaspoon vanilla extract

    Yellow food color

Beat butter until creamy. Gradually add powdered sugar and milk to butter, beating to desired consistency. Stir in vanilla and food color.

Hanukkah Coin Cookies

4 eggs, separated and at room
  temperature

½ cup plus ⅓ cup sugar,
  divided

1 teaspoon vanilla extract

½ cup all-purpose flour

¼ cup HERSHEY'S Cocoa

½ teaspoon baking powder

¼ teaspoon baking soda

⅛ teaspoon salt

⅓ cup water

  White Cream Filling
    (page 354)

  Chocolate Glaze
    (page 354)

CHOCOLATE AND WHITE YULE LOG

Makes 10 to 12 servings

1. Heat oven to 375°F. Line 15½×10½×1-inch jelly-roll pan with foil; generously grease foil.

2. Beat egg whites in large bowl until soft peaks form; gradually add ½ cup sugar, a tablespoon at a time, beating on high speed of mixer until stiff peaks form.

3. Beat egg yolks and vanilla in medium bowl on high speed about 3 minutes; gradually add remaining ⅓ cup sugar. Continue beating additional 2 minutes until mixture is thick and lemon-colored.

4. Stir together flour, cocoa, baking powder, baking soda and salt; gently fold into egg yolk mixture alternately with water just until mixture is smooth. Gradually fold chocolate mixture into egg whites; spread batter evenly into prepared pan.

5. Bake 12 to 15 minutes or until top springs back when touched lightly in center. Immediately loosen cake from edges of pan; invert onto linen towel sprinkled with powdered sugar. Carefully peel off foil. Immediately roll cake in towel starting from narrow end; place on wire rack. Cool completely.

6. Prepare White Cream Filling and Chocolate Glaze. Unroll cake; remove towel. Spread with filling; reroll cake. Spread Chocolate Glaze over top and sides. Cover; refrigerate until just before serving. Cover; refrigerate leftover dessert. *continued on page 354*

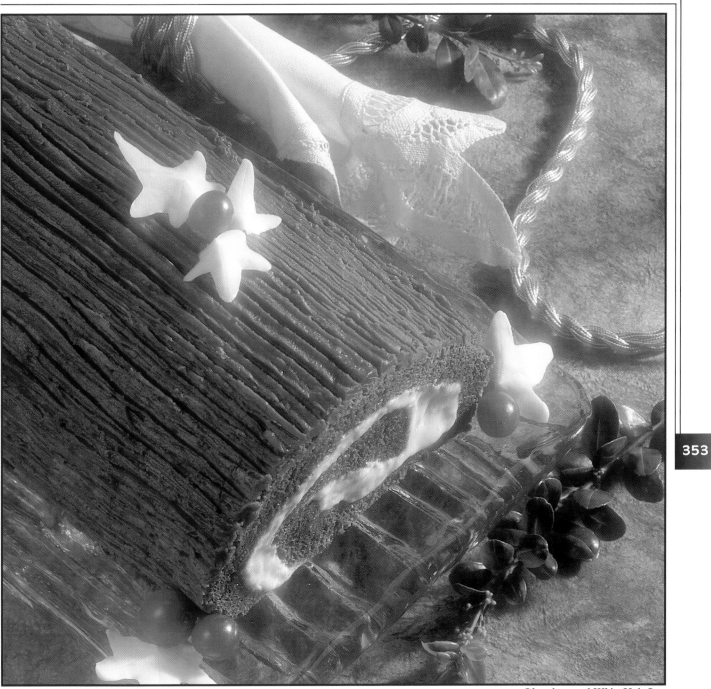

Chocolate and White Yule Log

HERSHEY, PA

COCOA AVE · CHOCOLATE AVE

CHRISTMAS IN HERSHEY

354

Chocolate and White Yule Log, continued

WHITE CREAM FILLING

Makes about 2 cups filling

- ½ **teaspoon unflavored gelatin**
- 1 **tablespoon cold water**
- ⅔ **cup HERSHEY'S Premier White Chips**
- ¼ **cup milk**
- 1 **teaspoon vanilla extract**
- 1 **cup (½ pint) cold whipping cream**

1. Sprinkle gelatin over cold water in small cup; let stand one minute to soften.

2. Combine white chips and milk in small microwave-safe bowl. Microwave at HIGH (100%) 30 seconds to 1 minute; stir after 30 seconds, until chips are melted and mixture is smooth when stirred. Add gelatin mixture and vanilla; stir until gelatin is dissolved. Cool to room temperature.

3. Beat whipping cream in small bowl until stiff; carefully fold into chip mixture. Refrigerate 10 minutes or until filling begins to set.

CHOCOLATE GLAZE: Melt 2 tablespoons butter or margarine in small saucepan over low heat; add 2 tablespoons HERSHEY'S Cocoa and 2 tablespoons water, stirring until smooth and slightly thickened. Do not boil. Remove from heat; cool slightly. Gradually add 1 cup powdered sugar and ¹/₂ teaspoon vanilla extract; beat with whisk until smooth. If necessary, add additional water, a few drops at a time, until of desired consistency. Makes about ²/₃ cup.

2½ cups (about 12 ounces) mixed dried fruits such as apples, apricots, pears and prunes

1¼ cups (8 ounces) dried Mission figs

1 cup MOUNDS Sweetened Coconut Flakes

½ cup HERSHEY'S Cocoa

2 tablespoons orange juice

2 tablespoons honey

1 cup HERSHEY'S Semi-Sweet Chocolate Chips *or* HERSHEY'S Milk Chocolate Chips

1 tablespoon shortening (do not use butter, margarine, spread or oil)

COCOA FRUIT LOG

Makes 32 servings

1. Remove pits from prunes and stems from figs, if necessary. Using metal blade of food processor, process dried fruits, figs, and coconut until ground and almost paste-like (or put through fine blade of food grinder.)

2. Combine cocoa, orange juice and honey with fruit mixture in large bowl; mix well. Divide mixture in half. Shape each half into a roll about 2 inches in diameter and 8 inches long; wrap in plastic wrap. Refrigerate until firm.

3. Place chocolate chips and shortening in small microwave-safe bowl. Microwave at HIGH (100%) 1 minute; stir. Microwave at HIGH additional 30 seconds or until melted and smooth when stirred. Place log on wax paper-covered tray; spread half of melted chocolate onto each log. Draw spatula through chocolate to form bark-like texture. Refrigerate until chocolate is set; store in airtight container. Cut into slices.

NOTE: Mixture can be shaped into 1¼-inch balls. Omit chocolate coating; roll in chopped nuts or powdered sugar before refrigerating.

355

1½ teaspoons baking soda

1 cup buttermilk or sour milk*

¾ cup HERSHEY'S Cocoa

¾ cup boiling water

¼ cup (½ stick) butter or margarine, softened

¼ cup shortening

2 cups sugar

2 eggs

1 teaspoon vanilla extract

⅛ teaspoon salt

1¾ cups all-purpose flour

Eggnog Sauce (recipe follows)

To sour milk: Use 1 tablespoon white vinegar plus milk to equal 1 cup.

CHOCOLATE CAKE SQUARES WITH EGGNOG SAUCE

Makes 12 to 15 servings

1. Heat oven to 350°F. Grease and flour 13×9×2-inch baking pan. Stir baking soda into buttermilk in medium bowl; set aside. Stir together cocoa and water until smooth; set aside.

2. Beat butter, shortening and sugar in large bowl until creamy. Add eggs, vanilla and salt; beat well. Add buttermilk mixture alternately with flour to butter mixture, beating until blended. Add cocoa mixture; blend thoroughly. Pour batter into prepared pan. Bake 40 to 45 minutes or until wooden pick inserted in center comes out clean. Cool completely. Serve with Eggnog Sauce.

EGGNOG SAUCE

Makes about 1³/₄ cups sauce

1 tablespoon cornstarch

2 tablespoons cold water

1⅓ cups milk

¼ cup sugar

3 egg yolks, beaten

¼ teaspoon each brandy and vanilla extracts

Several dashes ground nutmeg

Stir cornstarch and water in saucepan until smooth. Add milk, sugar and egg yolks. Beat with whisk until well blended. Cook over medium heat, stirring constantly, until thickened. Remove from heat. Stir in extracts. Cool completely. Sprinkle nutmeg over top.

357

Chocolate Cake Square with Eggnog Sauce

- 1 cup (2 sticks) butter or margarine
- ¾ cup HERSHEY'S Cocoa *or* HERSHEY'S Dutch Processed Cocoa
- 2 cups sugar
- 4 eggs
- 1½ cups plus ⅓ cup all-purpose flour, divided
- ⅓ cup chopped almonds
- 1 can (14 ounces) sweetened condensed milk (not evaporated milk)
- ½ teaspoon almond extract
- 1 cup HERSHEY'S MINI KISSES Semi-Sweet *or* Milk Chocolate Baking Pieces
- 1 cup chopped maraschino cherries, drained

CHOCOLATE CHERRY BARS

Makes about 48 bars

1. Heat oven to 350°F. Generously grease 13×9×2-inch baking pan.

2. Melt butter in large saucepan over low heat; stir in cocoa until smooth. Remove from heat. Add sugar, 3 eggs, 1½ cups flour and almonds; mix well. Pour into prepared pan. Bake 20 minutes.

3. Meanwhile, whisk together remaining 1 egg, remaining ⅓ cup flour, sweetened condensed milk and almond extract. Pour over baked layer; sprinkle Mini Kisses and cherries over top. Return to oven.

4. Bake additional 20 to 25 minutes or until set and edges are golden brown. Cool completely in pan on wire rack. Refrigerate until cold, 6 hours or overnight. Cut into bars. Cover; refrigerate leftover bars.

Chocolate Cherry Bars

4 eggs, separated

½ cup granulated sugar

1 teaspoon vanilla extract

⅓ cup granulated sugar

½ cup all-purpose flour

⅓ cup HERSHEY'S Cocoa

¼ teaspoon baking powder

¼ teaspoon baking soda

⅛ teaspoon salt

⅓ cup water

Powdered sugar

1 can (21 ounces) cherry pie filling, divided

1½ cups whipped topping

Chocolate Glaze (page 362)

CHOCOLATE CHERRY CREAM-FILLED LOG

Makes 10 to 12 servings

1. Heat oven to 375°F. Line $15^{1}/_{2} \times 10^{1}/_{2} \times ^{1}/_{2}$-inch jelly-roll pan with foil; generously grease foil.

2. Beat egg whites in large bowl until foamy; gradually add $^{1}/_{2}$ cup granulated sugar, beating until stiff peaks form.

3. Beat egg yolks and vanilla in small bowl on high speed of mixer for about 3 minutes. Gradually add $^{1}/_{3}$ cup granulated sugar; continue beating 2 minutes. Combine flour, cocoa, baking powder, baking soda and salt; add to egg yolk mixture alternately with water on low speed, beating just until batter is smooth.

4. Fold chocolate mixture gradually into egg whites; spread evenly into prepared pan.

5. Bake 12 to 15 minutes or until top springs back when touched lightly in center. Immediately loosen cake from edges of pan; invert on towel sprinkled with powdered sugar. Carefully remove foil. Immediately roll cake in towel, starting from narrow end; place on wire rack to cool.

6. Combine 1 cup pie filling and whipped topping; mix well. Unroll cake; remove towel. Spread with filling; reroll cake.

7. Prepare Chocolate Glaze; drizzle over top, allowing to run down sides of cake. Refrigerate several hours. Just before serving, spoon $^{1}/_{2}$ cup pie filling over cake. Serve with remaining pie filling. *continued on page 362*

Chocolate Cherry Cream–Filled Log

Chocolate Cherry Cream-Filled Log, continued

CHOCOLATE GLAZE

   2 tablespoons butter or margarine

   2 tablespoons HERSHEY'S Cocoa

   2 tablespoons water

   1 cup powdered sugar

   ½ teaspoon vanilla extract

1. Melt butter in small saucepan over low heat. Add cocoa and water. Cook, stirring constantly, until smooth and slightly thickened. Do not boil.

2. Remove from heat; cool slightly. Gradually blend in sugar and vanilla.

CHOCOLATE CHIP NOUGAT

Makes about 12 dozen pieces

   3 cups sugar, divided

   ⅔ cup plus 1¼ cups light corn syrup, divided

   2 tablespoons water

   ¼ cup egg whites (about 2 large), at room temperature

   ¼ cup (½ stick) butter or margarine, melted

   2 teaspoons vanilla extract

   2 cups chopped walnuts

   ¼ teaspoon red food color (optional)

   1 cup HERSHEY'S MINI CHIPS Semi-Sweet Chocolate *or* HERSHEY'S Semi-Sweet Chocolate Chips

1. Line 15½×10½×1-inch jelly-roll pan with foil; butter foil.

2. Combine 1 cup sugar, ⅔ cup corn syrup and water in a small saucepan; cook over medium heat, stirring constantly, until sugar dissolves. Continue cooking, without stirring. When mixture reaches 230°F on candy thermometer, continue cooking, but start to beat egg whites.

3. Beat egg whites in large bowl with mixer until stiff, but not dry. Continue cooking syrup until mixture reaches 238°F (soft-ball stage) or when syrup, dropped into small amount of very cold water, forms a soft ball which flattens when removed from water. (Bulb of candy thermometer should not rest on bottom of saucepan.) Remove from heat. Gradually pour hot mixture in a thin stream over whites, beating on high speed. Continue beating 4 to 5 minutes or until mixture becomes very thick. Cover; set aside.

4. Stir together remaining 2 cups sugar and remaining 1¼ cups corn syrup in heavy medium-size saucepan. Cook over medium heat, stirring constantly, until sugar dissolves. Cook, without stirring, to 275°F (soft-crack stage), or until syrup, when dropped into very cold water, separates into threads that are hard but not brittle. Immediately pour hot sugar mixture all at once over egg white mixture; blend with wooden spoon. Stir in butter and vanilla. Add walnuts; mix thoroughly. Stir in red food color, if desired.

5. Pour into prepared pan; sprinkle evenly with Mini Chips. Cool completely; do not disturb chips while cooling. Invert pan; remove foil. Cut into 1-inch pieces. Store in tightly covered container in cool, dry place.

1 cup HERSHEY'S Semi-Sweet
   Chocolate Chips, divided
½ cup sugar
¼ cup butter flavor shortening
¼ cup (½ stick) butter or
   margarine, softened
1 egg, separated
½ teaspoon vanilla extract
1 cup all-purpose flour
¼ teaspoon salt
1 cup finely chopped nuts

CHOCOLATE CHIPS THUMBPRINT COOKIES

Makes about 2½ dozen cookies

1. Heat oven to 350°F. Lightly grease cookie sheet. Place ¼ cup chocolate chips in small microwave-safe bowl. Microwave at HIGH (100%) 20 to 30 seconds or just until chocolate is melted and smooth when stirred; set aside to cool slightly.

2. Combine sugar, shortening, butter, reserved melted chocolate, egg yolk and vanilla; beat until well blended. Stir in flour and salt. Shape dough into 1-inch balls. With fork, slightly beat egg white. Dip each ball into egg white; roll in nuts to coat. Place about 1 inch apart on ungreased cookie sheet. Press center of each cookie with thumb to make indentation.

3. Bake 10 to 12 minutes or until set. Remove from oven; immediately place several chocolate chips in center of each cookie. Carefully remove from cookie sheet to wire racks. After several minutes, swirl melted chocolate in each thumbprint. Cool completely.

Chocolate Chips Thumbprint Cookies

½ cup (1 stick) butter or margarine

1⅔ cups (10-ounce package) HERSHEY'S Premier White Chips, divided

2 eggs

¼ cup granulated sugar

1¼ cups all-purpose flour

⅓ cup orange juice

¾ cup cranberries, chopped

¼ cup chopped dried apricots

½ cup coarsely chopped nuts

¼ cup packed light brown sugar

Festive Fruited White Chip Blondies

Makes about 16 bars

1. Heat oven to 325°F. Grease and flour 9-inch square baking pan.

2. Melt butter in medium saucepan; stir in 1 cup white chips. In large bowl, beat eggs until foamy. Add granulated sugar; beat until thick and pale yellow in color. Add flour, orange juice and white chip mixture; beat just until combined. Spread one-half of batter, about $1^{1}/_{4}$ cups, into prepared pan.

3. Bake 15 minutes or until edges are lightly browned; remove from oven.

4. Stir cranberries, apricots and remaining $^{2}/_{3}$ cup white chips into remaining one-half of batter; spread over top of hot baked mixture. Stir together nuts and brown sugar; sprinkle over top.

5. Bake 25 to 30 minutes or until edges are lightly browned. Cool completely in pan on wire rack. Cut into bars.

Festive Fruited White Chip Blondies

1 cup (2 sticks) butter or
     margarine, softened

1 cup sugar

1 egg

½ teaspoon almond extract

½ teaspoon vanilla extract

2 cups all-purpose flour

½ cup HERSHEY'S Cocoa

¼ teaspoon baking powder

¼ teaspoon baking soda

⅛ teaspoon salt

1 cup HERSHEY'S MINI CHIPS
     Semi-Sweet Chocolate

Additional sugar

Slivered blanched almonds

CHOCOLATE ALMOND COOKIES

Makes about 3½ dozen cookies

1. Beat butter and 1 cup sugar in large bowl until fluffy. Add egg, almond and vanilla extracts; beat well. Combine flour, cocoa, baking powder, baking soda and salt; gradually add to butter mixture, beating to form smooth dough. Stir in Mini Chips. If necessary, refrigerate dough about 1 hour or until firm enough to handle.

2. Heat oven to 350°F. Shape dough into $1^{1}/_{8}$-inch balls; roll in sugar. Place about 2 inches apart on ungreased cookie sheet. Place three slivered almonds on top of each ball; press slightly.

3. Bake 9 to 10 minutes or until set. Cool slightly. Remove from cookie sheet to wire racks. Cool completely.

Chocolate Almond Cookies

1 cup (2 sticks) butter or
    margarine, softened
1 cup sugar
2 eggs
2 teaspoons vanilla extract
2½ cups all-purpose flour
½ teaspoon baking powder
½ teaspoon salt
    HERSHEY'S Holiday Candy
    Coated Bits

HOLIDAY BITS CUTOUT COOKIES
Makes about 3¹/₂ dozen cookies

1. Beat butter, sugar, eggs and vanilla in large bowl on low speed of mixer just until blended. Stir together flour, baking powder and salt; add to butter mixture, stirring until well blended.

2. Divide dough in half. Cover; refrigerate 1 to 2 hours or until firm enough to handle. Heat oven to 400°F. On lightly floured surface, roll each half of the dough to about $1/4$ inch thick.

3. Cut into trees, wreaths, stars or other shapes with $2^1/_2$-inch cookie cutters. Place on ungreased cookie sheet. Press candy coated bits into cutouts.

4. Bake 6 to 8 minutes or until edges are firm and bottoms are very lightly browned. Remove from cookie sheet to wire racks. Cool completely.

TIP: Brownies, bars and cookies make great gifts. Place them in a paper-lined tin or on a decorative plate covered with plastic wrap and tied with colorful ribbon. For a special touch, include the recipe.

Prep Time: 30 minutes
Bake Time: 6 minutes
Cool Time: 1 hour

Holiday Bits Cutout Cookies

¾ cup (1½ sticks) butter or margarine, melted

1½ cups sugar

1½ teaspoons vanilla extract

3 eggs

¾ cup all-purpose flour

½ cup HERSHEY'S Cocoa

½ teaspoon baking powder

¼ teaspoon salt

⅔ cup chopped pecans (optional)

Chocolate Cream (recipe follows)

Assorted fresh fruit (banana, mango, papaya, peaches, pineapple or strawberries), sliced or cut up

COLORFUL KWANZAA BROWNIES

Makes 12 to 15 servings

1. Heat oven to 350°F. Grease 12-inch round pizza pan or 13×9×2-inch baking pan.

2. Combine butter, sugar and vanilla in large bowl. Add eggs; beat well with spoon. Combine flour, cocoa, baking powder and salt; gradually stir into egg mixture until blended. Stir in pecans, if desired. Spread batter into prepared pan.

3. Bake 20 to 22 minutes or until top springs back when touched lightly in center. Cool completely. Spread Chocolate Cream over top. Refrigerate about 30 minutes. Garnish with fruit just before serving. Store covered in refrigerator without fruit topping.

CHOCOLATE CREAM

Makes about 1 cup

1 package (8 ounces) cream cheese, softened

½ cup sugar

3 tablespoons HERSHEY'S Cocoa

1 tablespoon milk

1½ teaspoons vanilla extract

Beat all ingredients in bowl until smooth.

Colorful Kwanzaa Brownies

1⅔ cups (10-ounce package) REESE'S Peanut Butter Chips

¾ cup (1½ sticks) butter or margarine, softened

1 cup packed light brown sugar

1 cup dark corn syrup

2 eggs

5 cups all-purpose flour

1 teaspoon baking soda

½ teaspoon ground cinnamon

¼ teaspoon ground ginger

¼ teaspoon salt

JOLLY PEANUT BUTTER GINGERBREAD COOKIES

Makes about 6 dozen cookies

1. Place peanut butter chips in small microwave-safe bowl. Microwave at HIGH (100%) 1 to 2 minutes or until chips are melted when stirred. Beat melted peanut butter chips and butter in large bowl until well blended. Add brown sugar, corn syrup and eggs; beat until fluffy. Stir together flour, baking soda, cinnamon, ginger and salt. Add half of flour mixture to butter mixture; beat on low speed of mixer until smooth. With wooden spoon, stir in remaining flour mixture until well blended. Divide into thirds; wrap each in plastic wrap. Refrigerate at least 1 hour or until dough is firm enough to roll.

2. Heat oven to 325°F.

3. Roll 1 dough portion at a time to ⅛-inch thickness on lightly floured surface; with floured cookie cutters, cut into holiday shapes. Place on ungreased cookie sheet.

4. Bake 10 to 12 minutes or until set and lightly browned. Cool slightly; remove from cookie sheet to wire racks. Cool completely. Frost and decorate as desired.

377

VOLUME MEASUREMENTS (dry)

$1/8$ teaspoon = 0.5 mL
$1/4$ teaspoon = 1 mL
$1/2$ teaspoon = 2 mL
$3/4$ teaspoon = 4 mL
1 teaspoon = 5 mL
1 tablespoon = 15 mL
2 tablespoons = 30 mL
$1/4$ cup = 60 mL
$1/3$ cup = 75 mL
$1/2$ cup = 125 mL
$2/3$ cup = 150 mL
$3/4$ cup = 175 mL
1 cup = 250 mL
2 cups = 1 pint = 500 mL
3 cups = 750 mL
4 cups = 1 quart = 1 L

VOLUME MEASUREMENTS (fluid)

1 fluid ounce (2 tablespoons) = 30 mL
4 fluid ounces ($1/2$ cup) = 125 mL
8 fluid ounces (1 cup) = 250 mL
12 fluid ounces ($1 1/2$ cups) = 375 mL
16 fluid ounces (2 cups) = 500 mL

WEIGHTS (mass)

$1/2$ ounce = 15 g
1 ounce = 30 g
3 ounces = 90 g
4 ounces = 120 g
8 ounces = 225 g
10 ounces = 285 g
12 ounces = 360 g
16 ounces = 1 pound = 450 g

DIMENSIONS

$1/16$ inch = 2 mm
$1/8$ inch = 3 mm
$1/4$ inch = 6 mm
$1/2$ inch = 1.5 cm
$3/4$ inch = 2 cm
1 inch = 2.5 cm

OVEN TEMPERATURES

250°F = 120°C
275°F = 140°C
300°F = 150°C
325°F = 160°C
350°F = 180°C
375°F = 190°C
400°F = 200°C
425°F = 220°C
450°F = 230°C

BAKING PAN SIZES

Utensil	Size in Inches/Quarts	Metric Volume	Size in Centimeters
Baking or Cake Pan (square or rectangular)	8×8×2	2 L	20×20×5
	9×9×2	2.5 L	23×23×5
	12×8×2	3 L	30×20×5
	13×9×2	3.5 L	33×23×5
Loaf Pan	8×4×3	1.5 L	20×10×7
	9×5×3	2 L	23×13×7
Round Layer Cake Pan	8×1½	1.2 L	20×4
	9×1½	1.5 L	23×4
Pie Plate	8×1¼	750 mL	20×3
	9×1¼	1 L	23×3
Baking Dish or Casserole	1 quart	1 L	—
	1½ quart	1.5 L	—
	2 quart	2 L	—